Journey to Joy

Mary Renouf

Faithbuilders Publishing Limited
12 Dukes Court, Bognor Road
Chichester
PO19 8FX
United Kingdom

Tel: 01932 845 296
E-Mail: editor@faithbuilderspublishing.com
www. faithbuilderspublishing.com

First Published in United Kingdom, 2020

British Library Cataloguing-in-Publication Data. A catalogue record for this book is available from the British Library

ISBN: 978-1-913181-42-0
Cover Design & Typeset by Faithbuilders Publishing Limited
Cover photograph © Jane Jarvis. Used with permission.
Printed in the United Kingdom

Contents

Acknowledgements

I want to thank everyone who has played a part in this incredible journey of trust and faith in the Lord Jesus Christ, healing both physical and mental, leading to unbelievable joy. There are so many people who have played a part along the way to whom I will be eternally grateful.

Thank you to the Goldstone Church, especially Steve Waterton for the time he spent in prayer and believing we have a God who heals. As Steve was on the phone to me one day, I heard the audible voice of God saying "It is finished". Steve also spoke to me about being a Mary and not a Martha, which had such a big impact on my journey. He also gave me the scripture from Jeremiah 33:6 telling me to insert my name in that verse as though God was speaking to me. I had a sense this word was from God and finally found healing from the effects of the cancer and its treatment.

Thank you to Wendy Beck who through her obedience to the Holy Spirit prayed with me every week for a year and shared the challenges God gave her for me.

Thank you to the friends who supported me when Michael was sick, especially Sue Nightingale who, after Michael died, would use her one day off a week to go out for a coffee and to walk along the foreshore with me. No one will ever know how important those times were. They helped to keep me going through the black times of not having Michael and doing life on my own for the first time.

Thank you to Jacquie Muzzall for her support when I returned to the UK on my own, for having me to stay and helping me on my journey to finding a home and starting to put life back together again.

Thank you to Mary Austin who helped me make a start with writing this book by encouraging me to put in date order all the bits of paper where I had written down significant words and events, then to start recording them on the computer. It was as I did this that I was able to begin putting flesh on my story and the content started to flow. Mary then rearranged some of what I had written. I have learnt so much from Mary's input as I have continued on this journey.

Thank you to the friends at Lifespring Church for their help and support as I went through the years of grieving, for accepting me as I was, allowing me to cry and to let out the grief; for Sue Jameson's help and encouragement; for Patsy Cade who has given so much time to proofreading the book and has been such an encourager. She also helped with the study questions at the back of the book. Thanks to Marjorie Cannadine who has also been a great source of encouragement as we have walked and talked together.

I would also like to thank my children who have travelled parts of this journey with me, but especially Michael, who was my support for so many years, through the ups and downs that have marked my life and has now equipped me to continue this next part on my own.

There are so many more friends and family that have been a great encouragement and support to me on the journey. Each one of you have played your part in different ways helping me along on this journey to health and healing. A big 'thank you' to each one for the part you played.

Most importantly, I want to dedicate this book to the Lord Jesus Christ, without whose presence and Holy Spirit there wouldn't be a story to tell.

Reviews

In her book JOURNEY TO JOY, Mary Renouf has shown that it is possible to live an overcoming life, by God's grace, in all of life's circumstances.

It is written in a compulsive pacey style and as each event and situation unfolds we see a demonstration of Romans 8:28. *'And we know that God causes everything to work together for the good of those who love God, and are called according to his purpose for them.'* (NLT)

Mary has lived through several experiences of life that many battle with. Rejection, anxiety, fears, uncertainties, and the most painful of all, the death of her husband.

As her story unfolds, each episode reveals both pains, and overcoming, bringing her through to a place of confidence in the Fathering love of God. The narrative justifies the book's title.

I have had the privilege of seeing Mary walk through the last years of this journey and her testimony has real credibility.

The study guide at the end of the book has some thought-provoking questions which would be useful in small group discussion.

Mary Renouf demonstrates that anyone, by God's grace can be a hero of the faith.

Dave Fellingham
musician, song writer and worship leader

****

My attention was caught from the first sentence of this lovely account of a woman's life, who has lived through the momentous years of post-war Britain to the present day. This is the same era as my own life so I found I was identifying with much of her history. Mary's vivid and fast-moving style makes it enthralling. But what many will find especially appealing is her honesty with regard to her dyslexia and sense of inferiority, and the grief when her little sister died which resulted in severe depression. Those were days when causes of depression were not much understood. It was a new found faith in Christ which eventually brought her healing.

Mike and Mary were a couple I came to know quite well, and I know this faith pervaded every part of their life. But I didn't know about her involvement with Girl's Brigade and her skills in sewing. But I did witness Mary's dogged determination to keep going in tough times, including her battle with cancer. Particularly inspiring is her account of her husband's illness and death and how she has dealt with, and is still dealing with, the whole issue of bereavement. I believe many who are walking this path will find this very valuable and enlightening. She writes with straightforward humility about how her dependence on God and his word have strengthened and sustained her, and have brought her through the valley of the shadow into new joy.

I hope this little book will become treasured by many.

Wendy Virgo
author of many books including: Influential Women, Leading Ladies and Life Issues; Studies in Titus for Women.

Early Days

The Second World War bomb missed Wandsworth Town Hall and instead descended on number 7 Alexandra Road, where newly married Mr and Mrs Burroughes were sleeping in the small ground-floor flat that they had rented only a few days before. Both were knocked unconscious. Shortly afterwards, three men found Mrs Burroughes wandering around the street in a state of shock. Her husband remained trapped under a wardrobe until he was released by members of the rescue services. To make matters worse, Mrs Burroughes missed the cup of tea that the Red Cross were serving to the victims and helpers. She was not happy about this as she loved her cups of tea.

Very early the following morning the couple stripped the bed and carried the sheets to a nearby bus stop where they waited for a bus to take them to Mrs Burroughes' mother's house on Elmsleigh Road. The driver of a passing police car thought it suspicious that two people should be transporting large bundles away from the recent bombing and stopped to make enquiries. When he learnt that the couple were unfortunate victims, not opportunistic thieves, and had no coupons to buy new sheets, he gave them a lift. You needed coupons to buy anything, including household goods and clothes, during the war and for years afterwards. Life was very hard for them, having now lost their home and belongings. They had only the clothes on their backs and the bed linen that they were carrying.

My father, Louis Leonard Burroughes, was born thirty-one years earlier, in December 1913. As a child he contracted polio and he spent most of his childhood in a wheelchair, or bath chair as they were then called. The doctors said that he would never walk or become a father, but through stubborn determination he proved them wrong on both counts. He was a quiet but strong, determined man with a gentle soul. He followed his brothers by training to become a butcher but when the Second World War broke out his disability exempted him from military service, so he joined the Home Guard, otherwise known as Dad's Army.

Dad was a lovely honest man and was brought up as a Christian. His own father used to preach at the Railway Mission and his ten children would attend church three times every Sunday. The children were expected to sit in the front row for the morning and evening services and also to attend Sunday School in the afternoon. The Sunday Sabbath was strictly a day of rest and even the Sunday lunch had to be prepared the day before. The children also had to clean and polish their shoes on a Saturday to avoid any unnecessary work on the Sunday.

As a young man Dad's faith was very strong and once a year he would make the big trip and cycle to the Keswick Christian Convention, which was over three hundred miles from home. This would have been a huge feat for anyone but for a young man with the limitations left by polio, it was nothing short of a miracle. As time went on his Christian beliefs became more private.

My mother, Winifred Joan Harford, was born in May 1923. She had a very hard childhood with a strict Victorian upbringing: 'Children should be seen and not heard'. Her mother was a very stern lady and was not to be messed with. I remember staying with my grandmother when I was a teenager. I had bought a ticket to go to a Cliff Richard concert but my grandmother was horrified that I could possibly attend such an event and made me take it back. I was devastated because Cliff Richard was my idol at the time. Back in those days you did not question anything an adult said. You just did as you were told.

When she was five years old, my mother contracted pneumonia. Her parents were allowed to visit her in hospital only once a week, which was a very frightening experience for such a young child. The family lived in London and her father owned a horse and cart from which he sold fruit and vegetables. It was a very hard way to make a living and they struggled to make ends meet. After school my mother would help her father on his rounds so there wasn't any time to just be a child. Her only sibling was a sister who was ten years her senior. Christian faith did not play any part in her life.

Mum met Dad during the war and they started dating while they were both working in a butcher's shop in Wandsworth. Both men and women needed to play their part in the war. Most of the men were expected to fight and the women filled their places in factories, shops and other necessary work. The married women were allowed to serve locally, so as a single female, Mum was destined to be sent further afield.

When Mum discovered that she was due to be posted to a munitions factory in the north of England, she and Dad had to make some crucial decisions. They brought their wedding date forward and on 18th June 1944 were married at St Faith's Church, East Hill, London. The bomb that destroyed their first home fell only a matter of weeks later – and Dad was more than just concussed by it. He always played down his physical injuries but it was actually the trauma of having their home bombed while they were asleep inside it that took its toll on his health. For the next two years he was unable to work and was forced to draw a pension.

The doctor, fearing that Dad would have a total breakdown, advised him to leave London, so they moved to Southwick on the south coast and lived with one of his sisters. About four months later I was on the way – which was quite a shock for a couple who had been told that they would never have children. They ended up with six! First me, and then Pat, Peter, John, Beryl and Sheila. No wonder Dad struggled to make enough money to keep the family going. But he was a fighter with a strong will and plenty of determination. When the war ended life was very hard. Jobs were in short supply and Dad had a limited income as the wages were low. He had a wife and family to support, not to mention a significant disability to overcome.

In September 1946 Pat was born, fourteen months after me. At birth she weighed only about six pounds and struggled to gain weight – a major problem in the 1940s. Mum had to feed her every three hours and each feed took ninety minutes. I don't remember anything of these times, but Dad said that I was strapped in the pram in the kitchen while Mum was trying to feed Pat. By the time I was five years old, my mother had three small children to cope with. Times were difficult for my parents; they didn't have the modern equipment that we have today.

We still needed ration books to purchase basic food items as they were in short supply. Supermarkets didn't exist and groceries were bought at the corner shop, fruit and vegetables at the greengrocer's, and bread at the bakers. Treats came much later and were sold in the sweet shop. There were no 'ready meals' – you got meat and two veg if you were lucky. And if you wanted to contact someone, you had to use the local telephone box, which could mean a long walk to the nearest one and the need to make sure that you had the necessary copper coins to pay for the call. There were no home or mobile phones, no fridges or freezers, no washing machines or dishwashers, no televisions, or computers. Recreation consisted of board games, books, garden activities, the radio and later a record player.

While I was still quite young, our neighbour, who was a lay preacher, offered to take us to Sunday School at the local Methodist church in Portland Road, Hove. My mother accepted her invitation, but I do not recall much about that time. All I can remember is attending the Girls' Guildry (later the Girl Brigade) up until the age of seven, marching around pillars as though we were soldiers.

Pat was much brighter than me academically and I always felt slow by comparison. At age five I started at Connaught Road Infant School where we were given spellings to bring home. I struggled to learn these but Pat, who was not even at school, would recite them easily because she had heard them so often when I was reciting them to my mother. Our class teacher was aptly called Miss Payne. She was small, with a loud booming voice, and I found her very scary and intimidating.

One memory that sticks in my mind is of having to learn the three times table. Every pupil's name was written up on the blackboard and when each of us had correctly recited it to the teacher, she rubbed our name off the board. I knew that I would never remember it, no matter how hard I tried, so in the break time I crept into the classroom and deleted my name from the blackboard. I knew Miss Payne would otherwise brand me stupid and make a big issue of it, something I could not cope with.

It was only when I was in my thirties that I learnt that I was dyslexic, which explained many of the problems and difficulties that I had through my early life. There was no understanding then about dyslexia so I, and many others, struggled to cope. Not wanting people to think that I was stupid, I became an expert at concealing my lack of ability, but this didn't do much for my self-confidence. It took me years to change my thinking about myself.

I was seven when we moved to Queen's Park Road in Brighton, where my father took over a butcher's shop. We lived above the shop and, as there was no separate front door, we had to walk through the sawdust-strewn shop to get to the living area at the back. We still did not have a TV but I remember watching the Queen's Coronation on a small television at the home of one of Dad's customers.

Pat and I shared bunk beds in a room where the plaster was crumbling off the wall. While we were in bed the two of us used to have snail races up our arms – until I decided that I did not like the feeling of having a snail against my skin. Pat had her snail on one of her arms and mine on the other arm.

When I was a young girl Mum started to teach me to sew and I seemed to excel more at practical tasks than academic ones. I started attending the Brownies and made a dress for myself which I submitted in a Brownie competition. At first, they did not believe that I had made the dress as I was only nine or ten years old and the dress was thought to be 'too good'. I still have that dress, which I never got to wear because I had grown too much by the time it was finished. Eventually, I won a first-class certificate for my sewing. Then, when I was in the Girl Guides, I gained a number of certificates for various sewing and craft works. While others at school were making basic aprons, I was stitching an eiderdown for my bed and a woollen coat, hat and leggings set for my baby sister, Beryl. I excelled in needlework but still lacked confidence in my own ability.

In those days no one thought it dangerous for young children to go off on their own, and my parents were no exception. So, on Saturday mornings, while they worked in the shop, Queen's Park in Brighton became our regular haunt. I was about eight, Pat was seven and Peter was three. The park was a fun place, until disaster struck. There was a steep slope to the side of the pond there and Peter slipped down into the water. Being so young we were terrified and did not know what to do. Fortunately, a man went in after him and pulled him out.

Then there were the Sunday afternoon treats, walking down to the seafront to get a three-penny ice cream cornet at Norton's café, followed by a tram ride back home. Ice cream was a real treat then.

We had some good holidays too. Before Beryl and Sheila were born, Mum, Dad and the four of us children would take two suitcases and board a bus to Brighton Station, followed by a train to Portsmouth harbour and a boat to the Isle of Wight, landing at the end of Ryde Pier. We then caught a tram down the pier, a bus to Newport, and finally another bus, arriving at Aunty Phoebe's house in Chale Green, near Ventnor. We did not go every year, but when we did we always had lots of fun. We would spend time on the boating lake at Ventnor and play crazy golf at Sandown. I remember sitting outside shelling freshly picked peas from Aunty Phoebe's garden. These were happy times – but to think of a family of six going on holiday for up to two weeks with just two suitcases seems ridiculous now.

My parents did not go to church but we were still sent to Sunday School each week. We attended St Luke's Church on Queen's Park Road and when we reached about eleven years old we were encouraged to attend confirmation classes. Being afraid that I would show myself up if I had to read aloud or learn and repeat Scriptures, I didn't attend. Pat was confirmed and on subsequent Sundays, when others took communion, I remained isolated in my seat, wishing that I could join them. This was a pattern that I would repeat throughout my life. It reflected a complete lack of confidence in myself and in my abilities.

In 1959, when I was fourteen, my sister Beryl was born. I felt like a little mother to her, and would feed and play with her. Then, before she was even one year old, she died suddenly from meningitis and viral pneumonia. I did not cope well with her death and blamed everyone else, in particular my mother and the doctor. In my grief I felt that *someone* must be to blame and I really struggled to make sense of what had happened.

There was no real family communication surrounding Beryl's death. That was how things were at the time. She died in the afternoon and it was only years later that my youngest brother told me that he was not told of Beryl's death until after breakfast the following morning. That's because my parents thought that it would be better to let him have a good night's sleep first. He was five and I remember seeing my Dad standing in the lounge telling him the sad news while trying hard to keep his emotions in check. No one then was allowed to show emotion and even my sister Pat was told, 'You cry too easily' when she was grieving over Beryl's death. There was little understanding about grief then and the family didn't know how to communicate in general. It was only at my insistence that my sister and I were allowed to travel in the funeral car. My brothers were taken to the service by a neighbour.

Family life was never the same after that. I remember lying on my bed and telling myself that I would never let anything affect me emotionally again. It was not a good move, as my inability to understand grief eventually resulted in over thirty years of depression.

Only recently have people started to speak out about topics such as depression, grief and mental health and recognise the devastating effect that grief can have. Even Prince Harry spoke publicly about the effect that his grief at losing his mother had on him for over twenty years. My parents in particular grew up in a time when feelings were not acknowledged or discussed and you just got on with it. Looking back, I now realise that no one will ever know the effect that Beryl's death had on Mum herself, who was probably suffering from depression and grief. Indeed, it was not until many years after Beryl's death that I was able to have conversations with my brothers and sisters about the impact that it had on us and how it affected us all in different ways.

I left school when I was fourteen and went to Brighton Art College for a one-year City and Guilds course in dressmaking and design. When I had completed the course, I was given an amazing job offer: to work with Hardy Amies, the Queen's dressmaker. My mother protested, saying that a young woman aged fifteen should not be living on her own in London. With hindsight this was probably the right decision as I still had no confidence in myself and would not have coped. Instead I started a job doing alterations in a local department store. I was working with a lot of older ladies and, as the junior, I surprised them with my ability. After a while I got bored and realised that I needed a bit more variety.

After Beryl's death my teenage years were explosive. I felt that Mum did not allow me the freedom to develop my own personality and opinions. Life in the 1960s was different from my mother's teenage years during the Second World War. She was not able to adapt to change and reacted negatively to my desire for the independence that any young person wants. I was rebellious at heart and on one occasion decided that I would go out dancing at the Regent Dance Hall. I tried to slip out of the window unnoticed, but my mother was standing outside pushing me back in with a broom. As the oldest in the family, I like to think I paved the way to give my siblings an easier ride.

When I was eighteen and Pat was seventeen we left home and shared a flat together so I got the independence that I had been craving. We enjoyed sharing the flat but both of us had separate busy social lives. Pat had been dating Ralph for two years and things between them were getting more serious. When she got engaged she returned to Mum and Dad's home so that she could save to get married. I then lodged in Hove with an older couple – the father and stepmother of a sailor called Michael.

It was now September 1964 and my landlord Mick had his son Michael visiting. For two years Michael had served in the Far East with the Royal Navy. While on leave he decided to visit his father for a weekend. During that time, we spent hours sitting at the kitchen table talking and getting on really well. I was invited to join the family for a day out in Margate on the Sunday as company for Michael. We had a really relaxed day together. He was a chain smoker, cigarettes being very cheap for navy personnel. I detested smoking but said nothing about it. However, in only two days he picked up on how I thought his habit was a waste of money. The next evening, we went out on our first date. He took me to the cinema, turned to me and said, 'This is my last cigarette.' He was true to his word. He never smoked again from that day. I must have made quite an impression on him as he suddenly extended his weekend stay to cover the remainder of his leave without saying a word to me. Who knows why he did that?!

Michael was then posted to St Vincent Royal Navy base in Gosport, where he joined the Navy staff team running a training base for new recruits. He worked mainly from Monday to Friday and then spent his weekends in Hove, where I was working in a photographic shop. Every Friday, after finishing his shift, he would catch the train from Portsmouth to Hove and then return to St Vincent via the milk train early the following Monday morning. Michael had a great sense of humour and would always manage to make me laugh. He was good fun to be around and his nature was very easy going and laid back. We would spend hours just chatting and laughing together.

My passion at this time was ballroom dancing and on Saturday nights Michael would accompany me to the Regent Dance Hall in Brighton. He could just about bluff and shuffle his way around the dance floor. Then, unbeknown to me, he started taking dancing lessons in Portsmouth during the week. Evidently, I was having quite an impact on him and he was keen to impress me.

One evening three months after we first met, Michael proposed to me in his usual laid-back way. He was sitting in a rocking chair. There was no grand gesture or even an attempt to get down on one knee. Instead he just casually asked me if I would marry him. Once he had secured a positive answer, I decided to go back to the family home while we saved for the wedding. I changed jobs and started working for my father in his butcher's shop.

The work was second nature to me because I had grown up making sausages, cutting up joints and serving customers. I earned the same as I did in the photographic shop but I was also saving on bus fares and paying only a token amount in rent.

In love, the first photo with Michael. 1964

Marriage

Now that we were engaged, Michael and I wanted to be together, but fifty miles and an hour-long train journey separated us, so we were forced to see each other only at weekends. It made sense to get married sooner rather than later, but unfortunately, I was still only twenty years old and back then you needed parental consent before the age of twenty-one. Dad understood our desire to get married as soon as we could and eventually managed to talk Mum round. Once she had agreed, we set the date for eight weeks later. It is amazing how quickly a wedding can be arranged! Pat had married seven months earlier, so I borrowed her dress and made two bridesmaids' dresses for £8.

The day arrived. 31st October 1965. I was so happy and eager to get to the church and marry Michael that my Dad had to keep telling me to slow down! We held the reception at the hotel/pub over the road from where we lived and the buffet lunch cost just £35. We had managed to save enough money to spend a week's honeymoon in a hotel in Devon. The weather in November could have been dreary, but I remember bright sunshine and days of happiness.

Michael was based in Gosport and our first home was a small bedsit in Southsea, with a living room/bedroom about three metres square plus a tiny kitchen. We came home from our honeymoon with £8 to our name and used it for the first week's housekeeping. Our possessions consisted mainly of wedding presents: saucepans, a cutlery set, a few towels and tea towels and a number of cheese boards. Things were not important to us. What mattered was being together and we were content with that.

After a short time, we were allocated a modern Navy flat in Portsmouth, so we moved from a little two-room bedsit to a fully furnished two-bedroom flat with a separate lounge and kitchen-diner.

It was a wonderful change, but after only three months of marriage Michael was posted away on HMS *Hermes* for a tour of duty that sent him around the world. For the next three years he was at sea more than at home and I was having to continually readjust to his absences and returns. At one point he was away for five months which, for a newly married couple, was very difficult. What helped during that long period was a trip to Malta. The Navy arranged for the wives to fly there for two weeks while HMS *Hermes* was docked in Valetta Harbour.

While Michael was away I had one aim: to earn as much money as I could to save towards a deposit for our own home. I got a job as a sewing machinist making underwear for Marks & Spencer. I was paid per garment, and since I was very fast I was able to earn good money, usually more than Michael. Together we focused on saving every penny that we could.

Michael had been in the Navy since he was fifteen years old. In 1967, after ten years in the Royal Navy, he decided that although he had enjoyed his seafaring days as a single man, this lifestyle as a married man did not work so well. He now wanted to spend his time at home with his wife. So after his three-year tour of duty on HMS *Hermes* he resigned and found a job selling commercial refrigeration. Sadly, the environment was cutthroat and he did not feel comfortable, so after a year he began working for the agency Manpower. They gave him a variety of jobs: house removals, taxi driving and office work. Eventually he became a full-time progress-chaser for the space and defence company Marconi. This involved ordering parts that would be assembled for the latest space project.

Two years later we bought our first house, a three-bedroom terrace. In the Portsmouth area the houses were mostly pre-1930s and mortgages on older properties were difficult to obtain. Happily we succeeded in this quest and then set to work making it our home. The house still had its original fittings and there were no kitchen units, just a random sink and draining board in a cupboard. When it came to furnishings, we had a picnic table and chairs, and a very old cooker that had been left in the house. We bought a new bed from a catalogue and paid for it in weekly instalments. We purchased a three-piece suite advertised on a notice board for £2.50 and a fridge for £5. For the time being we went without a freezer, washing machine, television and carpets but we were happy. We finally had our own place.

Now that we were married and more settled, we decided to start a family. Simon was born in January 1971, weighing 8.5 pounds. I enjoyed motherhood and it felt very natural to me. Our daughter Jane was born in May 1973 and she entered the world at a much more convenient 6 pounds! Michael's new status as a father had a huge impact on him. Suddenly he needed to support a wife and two small children.

After two years with Marconi, Michael resigned and joined Link Miles in Lancing, again as a progress-chaser. Almost immediately he realised that he had made a mistake. The work was similar but the workplace was fifty miles away and the working environment turned out to be unappealing. It was when we sold our home and moved to Lancing that things started to go wrong.

Home life up to the 1950s was generally characterised by lack of communication and our respective parents had struggled to communicate with us when we were children. With the advent of pop music and 'Flower Power' in the early 60s, teenagers began expressing their thoughts and feelings more freely. This was something that Michael and I just didn't know how to do – particularly when we were facing difficulties.

Michael would come home from work frustrated by a job that he did not like, and would shout at me. I would retaliate in the same way. One day I put the children in the car and drove off somewhere, anywhere. I just could not continue as things were. I felt that Michael was to blame but did not believe that divorce was the answer. Our marriage vows were 'till death do us part' and we both took them seriously. Based on what I had learnt in Sunday School about a God who cared for me, I prayed: 'I can't go on like this. Please help me'. I thought no more about it.

Much to my amazement, God answered my one-line prayer, but not as I had expected. In my eyes, Michael was the one who was behaving badly so God would have to change him, not me. The next time he came home from work and started shouting at me I calmly took a step back and asked why he was behaving like this. My lack of retaliation and composed response to him shocked even me. Then, for the first time he was honest and admitted how unhappy he was in his job, and how pressurised he felt with the responsibility of providing for his family. He was out of his depth and was struggling to cope. We had never communicated on this level before.

Michael's father was in the Army. His parents had lived in married quarters on Army bases but had divorced when he was about eight years old. They both remarried, his mother to another Army officer. Michael had lived with them, so there remained a strong Army influence around the home. His childhood seemed happy enough. He grew up playing on the Army assault courses but had no real example of how family life ran and how families communicated together.

He did not have any academic qualifications so he completed a questionnaire and was surprised to discover that with his military skills and Navy discipline, his preferred occupation was likely to be in the police force. He considered this option and concluded that it was way above him. I encouraged him to at least find out about the job. If he was offered it he did not have to take it if he didn't feel happy about it. However, once he had investigated the possibility, he applied and was accepted. He loved his new role and never looked back.

When Michael joined Sussex Police he had to take a pay cut and since we could not afford to stay in our Lancing house we moved to a cheaper, smaller property in Shoreham. Two years later, with the completion of his training and rise in salary, we were able to move to Southwick. Lucy, our youngest, was born in March 1977 and her weight matched that of her older brother, 8.5 pounds.

Not long after moving to Southwick I met Rosemary Thomson, who invited me to her house for coffee one morning. While we were sitting in her garden she started telling me a bit about herself and mentioned that she was attending a study group. My social communication skills were virtually nil but I just about managed to ask her what sort of group it was. 'It's a Bible study group,' she replied and, noting my interest, invited me to go along.

How was I going to answer? So great was my lack of self-worth that whenever I was in a group setting I felt fearful and inadequate. I had no conversation skills and knew that I would be totally out of my depth. If anyone spoke to me I'd only be able to give a yes or no answer. Besides, I was frightened that others would see the real me and my lack of intelligence and reject me outright. Surprisingly, I accepted the invitation, but with huge reservations.

Before I started going to the Bible study group I had assumed that I was a Christian. I had been brought up to go to Sunday School and knew the Bible stories. I believed that there was a God up in the sky somewhere and had sent my own children to Sunday School as part of their education. Although I lived around the corner from the Methodist church, I did not have the confidence to attend myself. Nevertheless, I realised that the members of this group were different. They did not gossip about each other or run others down. They were friendly and caring and had a joy and peace that was difficult to put your finger on. As time went on I found myself secretly wanting what they had.

I cannot say exactly when I became a Christian but I continued to go to the Bible study group and began attending Southwick Methodist Church. As I grew in my knowledge of God's Word I tried hard to put what I was learning into practice. This continued for the next four years, by which time God was starting to prompt me about declaring my faith publicly. In the Methodist Church this meant becoming a church member.

I discovered that I would have to stand at the front of the church and answer some questions about my trust in Jesus Christ. This was an enormous step for someone who always sat at the back and dreaded speaking in public. Nevertheless, I decided that I needed to go for it and reasoned that there would be far fewer people at a Sunday evening service. I was wrong. The particular service in August 1981 was the minister's final evening and the building was crammed with people who wanted to give him a great send-off. God has a sense of humour and must have been chuckling as I stood to speak.

Macramé was all the rage in the early 80s. It is the art of knotting string in patterns. The finished article is put round hanging baskets for the display of flowers. I really enjoyed making hanging basket holders, but homes can cope only with a certain number so I decided to set up a stall at Burgess Hill market on Wednesdays. I found out where to buy the materials direct and began to sell them both in the market and from home. I became so good at macramé that I was encouraged to start teaching it at official adult education classes. I was excited that I could bypass academic subjects and help others to use practical skills. To my horror I found out that in order to teach, I would have to do an academic training course, but I somehow bluffed my way through Stage 1 and bypassed Stage 2. Although I did not know it then, my problem was Dyslexia.

In October 1983 I was asked to restart a Girls' Brigade Company. I had attended Brownies and Guides as a girl, but not the Girls' Brigade. Anyway, I did my training and began recruiting. I realised that many of the girls' parents could not afford the uniforms, so I bought blazers from all the charity shops in the area and started making the tunics and skirts so that the parents could buy the uniforms a lot cheaper.

The uniform production line was the easy part for me. More challenging was the first monthly Church Parade. I suddenly realised that I would have to sit at the front of the church for this event. Even worse, every September at the beginning of the new academic year, the boys and girls had an enrolment ceremony, and I would be expected to stand up at the front and address the whole church congregation. If I had known this earlier, I would probably have refused the job. But God kept me taking small steps one at a time and I conquered the challenge with lots of prayer support from the Thursday morning Bible study group. Gradually I was learning to trust God for what I couldn't do in my own strength.

The Boys' Brigade was a very successful group. My son, Simon, enjoyed being in the Cubs, but when, at the age of eleven, he joined the Scouts, his enthusiasm waned. He tried the Boys' Brigade, with their greater sense of discipline, and loved it. Like many of the older boys, he particularly enjoyed playing in the brass band and marching around the streets before the monthly Church Parade.

By contrast the Girls' Brigade had a mixed reputation. It had once existed in the church but for various reasons its numbers had dwindled to the point where the company had ceased meeting. I appreciated enormously what my son was gaining from the Boys' Brigade – which is partly why I accepted the leadership role in the Girls' Brigade. For the next five years I ran the Girls' Brigade with a group of helpers, some of whom became officers with greater responsibility. Organisation was my gift, but I could not have fulfilled the role without this wonderful team. I never cease to be amazed at how God sorts things out, using my gift of organising and bringing others around me who have the gifts that I didn't have.

One Sunday evening I went to my first baptismal service with some ladies from the Thursday morning group. Frankly, I could not believe what I was seeing. Those wishing to be baptised publicly shared what Jesus had done for them and were then fully immersed in a large tank of water, coming up looking like drowned rats (as I thought at the time). I was impressed by their courage but decided that I could never be baptised. God had other ideas.

At another baptismal service a few months later, I began to feel quite ill. Then the words that we were singing just seemed to jump off the page at me: *Trust and obey, for there's no other way to be happy in Jesus, but to trust and obey.* I suddenly knew that God was calling me to be baptised – something that I could never do in my own strength. Surely the only way to trust Jesus was to be willing. 'OK, Lord,' I said, 'I'm willing.' That was the starting point. The next step was to speak to the minister and I initially bottled out of that. I finally spoke to him the following week and, with the support of the Thursday morning group, was baptised on 22nd January 1984. I assumed that now I had been baptised, I had somehow arrived. How wrong I was!

I found it difficult to believe that God could address me through his Word. I was used to being in control of my life so there wouldn't be much about me that needed to be changed, would there? Actually, yes, there would, and at times I struggled to cope when God spoke to me about something that he wanted me to address. He had to show me step by step what he could do through me and give me a purpose in my life. I can look back now and see the road that he marked out for me. And when I consider what he has done in the past, I can move towards the future with confidence.

In the meantime, I was using my administrative skills to get the Girls' Brigade involved in a number of significant activities that they would not otherwise have had the opportunity to take part in. One particularly enjoyable activity was camping under canvas, and this was one of the first things that I organised for the girls. I needed a camping permit so as part of my training to achieve this, I arranged a joint camp with another Girls' Brigade company. Our senior girls joined the rest of the seniors from the Sussex Division for a camp in Wales. These were exciting times both for them and for me as I gained valuable experience from the other Girls' Brigade officers.

During our regular weekly meetings, the girls were involved in marching, working towards badges for different skills and participating in practical activities – notably craft. They entered Sussex Divisional competitions and won the Allen West Cup for craft three years running. I was very proud of them. The younger girls entered a competition for craft and mime and came away with a shield. They had never won anything before. Indeed, after five years we had acquired a whole cabinet of trophies for various successful pursuits.

Eighteen months after beginning the Girls' Brigade company, I decided to start a Girls' Brigade band. Everyone laughed at us. That activity was reserved for the boys, and they had done well at it. We were mere females – but females who were determined to make our mark and prove them wrong. The idea seemed impossible. There was no one to teach the band, no instruments and no money to buy any. Nevertheless, I found a tutor and some instruments and the girls overcame the ridicule. Soon sixteen of them were regularly playing their instruments and joining other band members from the Brighton area in a Boys' and Girls' Brigade District Church Parade marching along Brighton seafront. Later they were invited to join the Boys'

Brigade on their pre-Church Parade march around Southwick. This was a huge step for the girls and they gained tremendous confidence.

The Girls' Brigade activities had a very positive effect on church numbers, which increased significantly. I should have been riding high on the success that the team and I were enjoying. The truth was that throughout my time with the Girls' Brigade I was struggling with depression. I tried hard to cover it up and thought that I had succeeded. But those who knew me, Michael included, were not so easily fooled.

Wedding Day, October 1965

Depressed but Fighting

It was September 1985 and I wanted to wave a magic wand and make the feelings of depression disappear. Alas, that did not happen. I visited a homeopathic doctor for a couple of sessions but he was unable to help me so I decided that God was the only answer. I started meeting up with two ladies from the church for prayer and it became apparent that the root of my depression lay in past rejection. The women encouraged me to pray for myself, which was hard, and pointed me to two verses in the Bible. The first was 2 Corinthians 5:17 *'Therefore, if anyone is in Christ, the new creation has come; the old has gone, the new is here!'* The second was Romans 8:28: *'And we know that in all things God works for the good of those who love him, who have been called according to his purpose.'*

At this time, I was finding my Bible reading notes particularly helpful. They spoke to me about the goal of a Christian: to become more like Jesus. I needed to imitate him. Although he was God, he lived as a servant. He was single-minded and had inner power. He depended solely on God and turned adverse situations into advantages. He expertly managed his time, avoided any hint of self-pity and forgave those who had hurt him. And his life was characterised by abundant overflowing peace and joy. In spite of this awareness, I somehow still expected the depression to disappear without too much effort – just lots of enthusiastic expectation.

In October I went to a Christian conference with great expectations, but nothing changed and I felt as though God had given up on me. I knew that healing would not come as a result of what I did for God, (being baptised and running a Girls' Brigade Company), but because of what I allowed him to do in me by way of changed attitudes. The problem was simple: which of my attitudes needed changing? I had always behaved in a certain way and did not know how to act differently. I was beginning to realise that I needed to stop passively accepting my depression and start battling against it. Only as I co-operated with God would things start to change.

People prayed that I would be cut free from rejection, and I attended church services hopeful that I would be healed. Still nothing happened. I felt low and abandoned; on the outside looking in. At one evening service I went forward for prayer and although I was not feeling like worshipping God, I forced myself to worship. The tears began to flow and I could not stop them. God's Spirit was at work but I was unable to discern what was going on. The fact was that when my little sister died I had vowed that nothing would ever affect me emotionally again. I was simply living out my vow and protecting myself from being hurt. God knew that my emotions had been locked up and crushed down for years and that I needed to cry out my sadness.

As I read my Bible I learnt the difference between duty and faith. I had been brought up to do the right thing and please others, which was the way I gained approval. Since I lacked self-worth, what others thought of me was important. But God wanted me to enjoy pleasing him. There was a world of difference between the two and I was rapidly learning what that was. As I read Ephesians 6:16 I realised that the shield of faith was designed to extinguish the fiery arrows aimed at me. Rather than try to battle against the depression, I simply needed to deploy faith against it.

By this time I had heard about the baptism in the Holy Spirit, but feared that I might go weird and out of control if I asked for it. Someone prayed that I might experience this gift from God and told me that tongues would be a sign that I had received it. I tried hard to speak in tongues on numerous occasions but failed. Then one evening I was at a church service where I really sensed God's presence. Caught up in the joy of worshipping him, I spoke two words in tongues. Had everything now changed for good? No, it hadn't, because the next day I spiralled down into the worst depression that I had ever experienced. It lasted all the following month. I was fighting what appeared to be a never-ending battle.

A week before Christmas I had to force myself to go to the ladies' Bible study group. I did not want to go because I feared the question: 'How are you?' After the meeting two of the women were walking home in my direction. When we arrived at my house we were still in mid-conversation – which seemed to go on forever! Finally, I decided that it would be more comfortable in a warm house and asked them if they would like to come inside for a cup of tea. To my surprise they said yes. I was more familiar with the answer, 'Sorry, no, I'm busy' or 'I need to be off'. They stayed until my daughter returned home from school and by then I was on top of the world. I actually felt accepted and the depression lifted.

The Christingle service, held on 24th December, was always a highlight in our church. It celebrated Jesus as the light of the world and was a great opportunity for whole families to come together. That year Michael and I invited everyone back to our home to celebrate. There must have been about twenty people present, including Girls' and Boys' Brigade children, parents and grandparents. Several close friends there realised that I had experienced a significant healing.

As we started the new year God was doing a lot in my life and giving me fresh confidence in myself. At a Girls' Brigade training weekend, I was amazed by how freely I was able to converse with the other officers. A new 'me' was clearly emerging. Slowly I was stepping out of my comfort zone, being willing to go forward for prayer at church services and asking for more of the Holy Spirit.

God worked on me bit by bit, like a great sculptor chiselling away at my character to make me more like Christ. He encouraged me from the Scriptures, pointing out that he disciplines those he loves and that discipline brings positive results (Hebrews 12:5–11). Like a master instructor he was breaking my pride and self-reliance and showing me that he loved me too much to leave me the way I was. In the environment in which I was brought up there was very little praise or encouragement and I was repeatedly told, 'You don't achieve anything except by your own efforts.' Unconsciously, I was locked into the same behaviour patterns, pushing myself to the limit and then getting overtired, with the inevitable lack of energy and sense of frustration. As I learnt how to rest in God's love, he revealed more and more to me and restored my self-worth.

Although God was moulding my character, I was still having medical problems. In May I was told that I needed a hysterectomy, which was scheduled for a few weeks later. I had great peace about it, but after the operation I suffered so much pain that I struggled even to hold a mug of tea. All I could do was sit on a sun lounger, read and enjoy the good weather. I was a very active person so I found this really difficult. It was a hard but humbling experience adjusting to being immobile and allowing others to do everything for me. But after five weeks the pain disappeared and the depression that was threatening to return lifted.

Nine weeks after my operation I ran my first Girls' Brigade camp – under supervision because I was still in training at this point. In the run-up to the event I had found some tents within our price range and some helpers to look after every aspect of the work. The girls had a brilliant seven days away and I was feeling great – first up in the morning and last to bed at night. The Lord was certainly looking after me, although the event tired me out and made me very grateful for a relaxing family holiday afterwards in our caravan in York.

When we returned home I sensed that God was speaking to me about selling the caravan. I really did not want to do this as I loved our caravan holidays and believed that they were the only way that we could afford to go away. Finally, with a fresh sense of peace, I decided to obey God and trust his judgment. I was surprised when Michael agreed to the plan, although he had no idea that God had been speaking to me about it. Had he known that, I might have received a different response as he was very anti-God at this time. We sold the caravan and the car, and were then able to buy a smaller, more economical vehicle.

With the new academic year came the new Girls' Brigade season, and the phone and doorbell never seemed to stop ringing. Happily, other people were now working with me so I was not under as much pressure as before. But then I took my eyes off God and got over-busy.

The depression returned and I was left wondering if I could carry on because everything seemed so pointless and black.

However hard it was, I was still attending the Thursday morning ladies' group, although I still lacked confidence and was unable to ask questions. As we went through a study book together God began to speak to me about sin. Until then I had always thought that sin related to vices such as murder, adultery or stealing, but God showed me that it also referred to attitudes like worrying, self-pity, complaining and bitterness. I had no trouble hanging on to these things as they were part of my character and I struggled to see them as wrong. God was challenging me to be transformed by the renewing of my mind (Romans 12:2). In a nutshell, I had to learn how to think differently.

Alas, some attitudes were buried so deep I was not aware that they were there and it took me a long time to recognise and deal with them. God brought them to mind gradually so that I would not be overwhelmed. I also learnt that depression involved allowing my thoughts to wander down comfortable and familiar pathways and turning a small difficulty into something out of control. It took firm determination to redirect my mind onto new routes, comply with God's Word and pray before depression dragged me off course.

Gradually I was learning to give everything to God and to trust that his answers were better than mine. This was easier said than done. While I longed to be free from depression, I was still grappling with past experiences and fears that threatened to hold me back. Eventually, I began to see the difficulties as a doorway through which I needed to step in order to experience a deeper understanding of God. Often I could have given up but I fought the negative thoughts, determined to keep my eyes on him. I was stunned by his response to my obedience.

I was aware that God was not only blessing me; he was also blessing my work. The Girls' Brigade company was really taking off. I was no longer leading everything alone. I had helpers to run the different age groups and activities, and Mr and Mrs Payne were doing an exceptional job with the band.

The Covenant Service starts a new year in the Methodist Church. In January 1987 it had a special significance for me. Usually I would look back and regret what I had not done, but that year I felt very excited. God had been doing a wonderful work in my life. Even after I had been a Christian for a number of years, it surprised me how much I had been influenced by my past and how others' opinions had affected me. *'No branch can bear fruit by itself; it must remain in the vine'* (John 15:4). I had read this Scripture many times, but now it jumped out at me. There was a pattern: God would reveal what needed changing, I would respond, he would draw closer and life would become more exciting.

I discovered that I could get more done if I started the day by reading the Scriptures and praying. It was not easy to do, but I desperately needed God's encouragement, especially when the depression and rejection threatened to overtake me. Some members of my wider family thought that I was some kind of religious nut and it was hard not to let their opinions affect me. But teaching from the Bible about discipline, forgiveness and not holding grudges helped to keep me positive.

On many occasions, I did not feel that God was speaking to me, but this changed as I started putting him first. One particular morning I spent time with him and then decided to do some home-orientated jobs before I went out. At this time I was finding it hard to stay at home on my own, so a decision to do just that was unusual. A friend then phoned. She said that she was having the worst day ever and needed to talk to someone. I invited her over, we chatted and she finally left two hours later, saying how much better she was feeling. I was feeling better too! That day I learnt a very important lesson: when life seems at its most mundane, God often orders our steps if we put him first.

Life still had its problems, of course, and the headmaster of the local school really frustrated me. My team would arrange a Girls' Brigade activity and he would almost deliberately organise some school event that conflicted with it: a sponsored spelling competition or a parents' evening. I would speak to him about this and he would respond with a good attitude, but then he seemed to do everything he could to make things as difficult as possible. My first reaction was to get angry. Then I recognised that this was a spiritual battle and simply prayed.

After hours of rehearsals, we joined with other girls from Sussex and took part in the Annual National Girls' Brigade Display at the Royal Albert Hall in London. This was such an honour, and there was a lot of excitement among many of the girls, who had probably never dreamt about such an auspicious opportunity.

In July I ran my first camp without supervision, although I had a brilliant team helping me. Much to my delight, the Girls' Brigade company was going from strength to strength, with membership increasing all the time.

In September we entered a float in the Southwick carnival – another first for the company and more excitement for the girls. The Girls' Brigade band also led the carnival. 'Count your blessings, name them one by one' goes the old hymn. Our blessings just kept coming: church parades, the Royal Albert Hall, our own camp, the girls' band leading a local carnival with our own float in it – all within a few weeks. I was still struggling with depression, but was also determined to put God first.

The Thursday Bible study group taught me about tithing. Money was tight but I wanted to obey God. Since Michael was not a Christian I decided that I could only tithe the income for which I was responsible, namely the housekeeping and family allowance. The surprising result of this was that when the conservatory was blown down in the October 1987 storm, we were able to replace it with a proper extension and, much to my amazement, furnish the interior too. There seemed to be an abundance of cash and even Michael himself was puzzled over where the resources had come from. There was no extra money coming in but somehow we seemed to have a bottomless bank account. It was another lesson in trusting God.

Actually, our own children and the young people at the Methodist church benefitted from the extension. They would often come around just to hang out and Michael enjoyed their company. When they failed their driving tests they would ask him, a police-trained driver, to help them. One lad failed three times but passed after Michael took him out on the road and gave him some advice. Another hit a lamp post and came to Michael for advice.

By this time there were about sixty Girls' Brigade members. In November God spoke to me from John 15:2, where we read that he prunes the vine to make it even more fruitful. As I prayed about this I sensed that God wanted me to pass the leadership of the company on to someone else. June 1988, the end of the Girls' Brigade year, seemed the best time to do this.

In May 1988, one month before I left, we were scheduled to take part in a district tambourine routine at the Royal Albert Hall. The prospect of a double-decker bus ride and the provision of all the costumes had an enormous impact on the girls, who demonstrated a heightened sense of excitement throughout the journey. It was an electrifying experience for everyone, and Michael and two other 'groupie' husbands came along to help and support us.

Leading the Girls' Brigade was a huge learning curve. I had done my best to take one step at a time and, with God's help, had overcome unfamiliar and challenging situations. Although difficult, my involvement had been highly momentous, so leaving it all behind was really hard, almost like a bereavement. I struggled to understand why God was removing me when things were going so well. But looking back I realised that my identity had started to lie in the Girls' Brigade's phenomenal success and that I was in danger of becoming proud of my achievements if I was not careful. God was taking me into a new phase. I needed to bow to his wisdom because he saw the bigger picture and I did not.

A New Season

It was not altogether easy living out my faith at home. Certainly, Michael was very supportive when it came to social events and Girls' Brigade activities, but for him Christianity was a joke and Christians were simply weak individuals who needed a crutch. Some believers seemed normal, while others struck him as being somewhat super-spiritual, without any interests other than church. He could not understand or relate to people who appeared to be far removed from the real world and his passion for music, the pub and snooker. Consequently, he was often scathing of them. Change was afoot, but I had to wait for it.

I began sensing that God was moving me on. I never cease to be amazed by how he works. A chance conversation with a friend changed my direction. She told me that while she was on holiday in Corfu someone had recommended Bishop Hannington Church in Hove because the teaching was good. I immediately felt a prompting to attend, so the next Sunday evening I visited and thought, 'This is the right church for me', although it was somewhat different from what I was looking for. I loved the Bible teaching, but only understood later how important that teaching would be for Michael.

In spite of his anti-Christian views, Michael was willing to come to the Christmas Carol Service, but not with a very positive attitude. His goal was to remain unmoved, to avoid singing any of the hymns and to 'stare the vicar out' during the sermon. I was sad that my ten-year battle in prayer for Michael had resulted in nothing but increasing hostility to the gospel message. Many others had prayed too but he was as angry as ever with Christians and did not have a good word to say about them.

I'd been struck by the Bible verse *'Ask and it will be given to you'* (Matthew 7:7) and had a strong sense that God wanted me to thank him for responding to my prayers when I still could not see the answers. In November my prayers for Michael's salvation changed to thanking God for answered prayer. When we went as a family to the Carol Service the following month, the music touched him more deeply than he expected and he was surprised when the preacher referred to the subject of sport in his address. The children noticed that Michael was actually singing the carols. They desperately wanted him to become a Christian and, on seeing his enthusiastic singing, kept nudging each another in excitement. This enthusiasm did not last though as Michael's negative attitude to Christianity returned and even seemed to get worse.

Spring Harvest is a week-long Christian event with praise and worship, Bible teaching, seminars and children's activities held at the Butlin's holiday resorts. In April 1990 a group of Christian friends arranged to go to Spring Harvest at Skegness. Naturally, Michael had no intention of joining us, but he had just bought a new car and said he was not keen on me driving the children such a distance without him; or more to the point, he did not trust me driving his precious vehicle! He therefore decided to be our chauffeur. Before we left he told my friends, Joan and Henry, that he was going very reluctantly and would be frequenting the bars (which he did not realise would nearly all be closed during the event) and taking a snooker cue and a large pair of wire cutters so that he could escape if necessary!

God has a wonderful sense of humour. Michael did not trust my driving, but ironically, he had an accident on the journey; his first and only one ever! We slowed down behind a queue of traffic and the driver behind us did the same, but the car behind her kept going and shunted her into us. At first, Michael was livid and his face said it all. The children and I just sat there looking at each other, not saying a word. We all knew how Michael was likely to behave. Then he noticed that one of the two women in the car behind was heavily pregnant and that the other had a two-year-old child. His police training kicked into action and he demonstrated great compassion. One thing Michael could not get over was the fact that a police motorcyclist suddenly appeared out of nowhere to deal with the situation. Fortunately, there were no serious injuries and the amazing thing was that our car had only the smallest of scratches. The one behind us, which was now concertina-shaped, was a complete write-off.

Once we arrived, our children, my friends and I were all in our element. Michael, on the other hand, was on a different sort of 'high'. He joined the 'low-profile' group, which was for those who weren't Christians or who were 'just looking'. By the third day he was leading a small band of three against the Christians in the group and was enjoying himself being as disruptive as possible and objecting to any Christian viewpoint that came up. I felt concerned by his attitude and voiced my alarm to Joan and Henry. Henry simply said 'Let's pray.' So as Michael went off to his group, a number of Christian friends gathered in one of the chalets to call on God for him. After a while, Henry made a startling announcement. With tears rolling down his face he suddenly declared, 'The Lord has got him. I've just "seen" Michael with a ring of light around him.' With that, everyone stopped praying.

I knew that when Michael became a Christian he would not have a Bible so, challenged by Henry's words, I immediately went and bought one for him, together with a cover to put it in and some Bible study notes for new believers. I hid everything in my suitcase. When Michael returned we all gathered for lunch and he started talking to one of the women, asking her questions about Christianity in a way that I had never heard him speak before.

That afternoon Michael said that he was going to another meeting but remained very vague about its purpose. I soon discovered that it was for people who wanted to know more about Christianity and I went with him to the venue to make sure that he arrived. He told me later that there was such a battle going on in his heart that he had not been able to go inside until he had walked all around the campsite first.

At the end of the day we met our friends for an evening drink and Michael was talking to the same lady again and asking her more questions. She listened to him and then said, 'From what I hear, you've already made a decision to follow Jesus.' He replied, 'Not at Spring

Harvest – there's too much hype!' But then he added 'Actually, I suppose I have made a decision. I just did not want to tell you here.' For ten years dozens of people had prayed for my husband and had endured his rudeness and hostility. It is hardly surprising, therefore, that we were all over the moon at his conversion. Our excitement knew no bounds!

Naturally, we were keen to share this miracle with our children and the church youth group. On our way I stopped off to get the Bible that I had bought and Michael wanted to know how I knew what had happened. Henry merely pointed to the sky and said, 'We've got a satellite link up there, Mike.'

The youth group on the campsite knew only too well how hostile Michael had been towards Christians so when he told them that he had given his life to Jesus they did not believe him. It took ages for Henry, Joan and me to convince them. Even one of my son's friends who was not at Spring Harvest later refused to believe the news until he had heard it from Michael himself. It is no wonder that Joan commented years later that his salvation was the biggest miracle she had seen in her seventy years as a Christian, and other Christians said the same.

On our journey back home, we stopped off at a Little Chef restaurant where Michael led a company of believers in a public rendition of the song 'Shine, Jesus, Shine'. Perhaps it was no wonder that the rumours of his conversion reached Southwick long before we got anywhere near Sussex ourselves. When we arrived Michael just said that he had to go out. Then, unbeknown to me, he visited many of my Christian friends and apologised for his behaviour to them in the past. Such was the shock of Michael's conversion that even the Shoreham Police Station superintendent came to Michael's office to find out what had happened.

Now, eighteen months after I had started attending Bishop Hannington Church, I could see why this was the place where God wanted me. It had to do with the fact that shortly after his conversion, Michael was invited to join a preachers' workshop. He did not have any personal aspirations in this direction and merely went along because he had been asked to. At the first meeting the group was informed that a small church congregation in the area needed weekly preachers. A list of required dates was handed round and Michael signed up. He chose the last preaching date to give himself the maximum amount of time for preparation. Then he took lots of advice and studied hard night after night, even abandoning the TV in the process.

Five months after Michael became a Christian he was baptised in the sea in Hove and the following month we celebrated our twenty-fifth wedding anniversary. We took the family to Orlando and had a really exciting two weeks. Michael was still on a post-conversion 'high' and the family spent a very happy holiday together. Understandably, I was thrilled at the changes in my husband and for eighteen months we enjoyed all kinds of spiritual and social activities together.

A year later Bishop Hannington Church started its first church plant, Goldstone Church, and Michael and I were the first people to join it. I served in a number of ways, but in spite of all the good things that were happening, I found myself struggling with depression again.

I still wanted to withdraw during our home group times, but at one meeting we were discussing the subject of fear and I suddenly realised that I was responding to others in the same way as I had reacted as a child. I had grown up with criticism and now I dared not say or do anything because I might be judged, left out or asked to do something that I could not cope with. My reluctance to speak or pray aloud now made complete sense. I just could not cope with any negative arrows that might be fired in my direction. This fear actually had an incredible hold over me. It made me physically unwell and was the cause of some severe chest pains.

The depression was very black and it was accompanied by a strong sense of rejection. I began seeing a friend who had some counselling experience, and a number of Christians from the Goldstone church also tried to help me. God began reminding me of various unhappy past experiences when I had been rebuffed, misunderstood or simply treated unfairly. My counsellor friend prayed through these things and Jesus often drew close to me and released me from their influence on my life.

A few friends also gathered to pray for me. I remember someone telling me that my problem was rooted in fear and that I should rest and soak in God's love. I hoped that he would immediately remove the depression. He did not do that. I was bitterly disappointed, received more prayer and was encouraged by some verses in Isaiah 43:18–19, which spoke about God beginning a new work and making a pathway through the wilderness. I was told that I needed to pray for boldness to overcome passivity and believe by faith that God would intervene.

My whole life seemed to be dominated by fear. I feared that if people knew the real me they would reject me. I feared their response to my perceived lack of intelligence. I feared coming out from behind my mask and admitting that I was depressed because of what they would say. I also struggled to believe that anyone could love me, most of all God. But God never gave up on me.

Over the next few weeks he highlighted my inability to feel love and emotion and give hugs to others. I sensed that he wanted me to spend more time reading the Bible and drawing closer to him. I needed to trust him and receive more of his love and his Spirit. So, encouraged by my friends, I gave my pain to God and surrendered these issues to him again. The result was quite stunning. I felt much better and more positive, had my first good night's sleep for two weeks and swam fourteen lengths at the local swimming pool!

God gave me a picture of light shining through trees. The light got steadily brighter until it was very intense and powerful. At first, I thought that he was telling me that he was going to lift the heaviness in me and give me a joyful heart. Later I sensed that I would be that light and that others would be attracted by it. Such prophetic words were new and unfamiliar to me at the time.

I had mixed emotions. I needed faith to believe what God could do, and trusting him was hard. The Bible says, *'Therefore humble yourselves under the mighty hand of God, that he may exalt you in due time, casting all your care upon him, for he cares for you'* (1 Peter 5:6–7 NKJV). I did my best to draw close to him and give him my fears and anxieties.

Christmas Day at home that year was punctuated by lots of laughter and fun. Neither Michael nor I came from families where communication was easy but we were working at it, even if for me the feelings of depression were always just around the corner.

In the summer of 1992 I was in the blackest of black depressions. The only thing that stopped me from committing suicide was the belief that God was the only one who had the right to take a life because he first gave it. I realise this may not be everyone's view but it was certainly mine. I phoned the leader of our church and he gave me some Scripture verses to consider.

I had no problem believing the Bible, but believing it for me was a different matter altogether – until then. Suddenly, I had the strong sense that God wanted me to trust that these verses were for me to appropriate, so I just said in my heart, 'I'll believe that these Scriptures are for me personally.' No sooner had I made up my mind to believe God's Word than I heard an audible voice declare, 'It is finished.' In fact, the voice was so clear that I turned around to see who it was, but I was alone. From that moment something just lifted off me and the depression ended.

God showed me I needed to change my thinking. Instead of allowing my thoughts to descend into negativity, I needed to focus on the truth of Scripture. I had to work hard at this because it took time and effort to correct years of wrong thinking. Nevertheless, as I responded to God, he met me, and my beliefs about myself, and consequently my behaviour, were transformed.

What's Up?

Books Alive was the Christian bookshop in Hove. I had been helping on a voluntary basis since the shop opened, so when the owner had an accident I was asked to step in and manage the shop during her time off. About eighteen months later it was sold to a local church and I was asked to continue as manager. This wasn't an easy task for someone who was unknowingly suffering from dyslexia, but I used my organisational gifts, which proved to be particularly helpful when the shop was undergoing a refit.

I built a relationship with Sue, whom I was training to do my job and be deputy manager. I shared with her the difficulties that I had with dyslexia so she took on the elements that I found hard and I used my strengths to manage the shop. Our partnership worked very well and our friendship has continued over the years, as has our mutual love for scrapbooking.

My eldest daughter, Jane, married Martin in May 1993, and at this time I was really enjoying life. I was feeling like a different person and was experiencing more emotional freedom than ever before.

In September the following year Michael and I went on holiday to the Greek island of Kos. As soon as we left home I started getting stomach pains but I put this down to excitement rather than illness. Unfortunately, the pains worsened and by the time I was on the plane I was vomiting after I had eaten and feeling faint and dizzy. I was so sick that I did not know what to do with myself. I'd been feeling unwell for about eighteen months but it was never as bad as this.

When we arrived in Kos I sat down on a kerb outside the airport because I thought that I was going to pass out. During our first night I got up to be sick and was in so much pain that I fell on the bathroom floor and writhed around in agony, totally unable to return to bed on my own. I just about managed to get through the rest of the holiday by restricting myself to a bland diet and minimal amounts of food.

One Saturday morning I was in the bookshop phoning around for some staff members to help me. This task was often difficult because most of my colleagues were volunteers with no obligation to work. The situation might not have presented such a problem had I been feeling well, but I was not. The toilet was upstairs and I went to work with a bucket because I was feeling physically sick and didn't think that I would make it upstairs in time.

Jane phoned me at the shop and was so concerned that she came and actually took over from me. I was so grateful. I showed her the basics and she did the job like a professional, although it normally took weeks to train new staff members. She phoned the doctor, who agreed to stay late to see me, and a customer drove me to the surgery, with bucket in tow. I was given a thorough examination but the doctor wasn't able to diagnose the cause of the high level of pain that I was experiencing or the reason for the sickness, so she sent me home with some strong painkillers and a referral letter.

I had always hated being the centre of attention and preferred to keep a low profile, but I was feeling so ill that I humbled myself and went to the church leadership to ask them to pray and anoint me with oil. The Bible tells us that if anyone is sick they should call the elders of the church to pray over them and anoint them with oil in the name of Jesus (James 5:14). They did this for me. That evening I went to a service at the Church of Christ the King (CCK) where John Arnott, a church leader from Canada, prayed for me. As soon as he had finished, I suffered the most incredible pain and was shaking all over. John returned, looked at me for some minutes and stated, 'You should visit your doctor.' I'd been to my GP so many times that I was reluctant to go again, but I followed his advice and was subsequently sent to the hospital for some X-rays. After viewing these, the doctor announced that I had gallstones.

Our main book supplier operated from a depot in Carlisle. Michael and I could not attend the booksellers' conference there because we were away in Kos, so we were invited to go when we returned. The staff laid on a wonderful spread of food for us, but I dared not eat any of it. I must have looked as ill as I felt because people expressed great concern at the state of my health. I was on extra-strong painkillers and by the time we arrived at our guest house I was in such agony that I had to ask for an appointment with the local doctor. Our hostess told us that the waiting time for appointments was usually about two weeks and she was amazed that I got one in half an hour with the best of the ten doctors in the practice. He looked at my eyes, questioned my colour, said that I looked jaundiced and arranged for an urgent blood test. Then he strongly advised me to phone back in a few hours for the result.

On our way home from Carlisle we stopped off in Birmingham to phone for the blood test results. There were no mobile phones then, so we stopped at a phone box and I scribbled down the information and asked what it meant. I was told that my haemoglobin level was 7.5 and that I needed to see my own doctor as a matter of urgency. I immediately phoned my GP to request an appointment. I got this and attended the surgery within minutes of our return – another abnormal occurrence.

My doctor noted the blood test results and was amazed that I was still working full-time. She signed me off work and said that she would be in contact. The following morning, she phoned me at 8:30am with an appointment to see a consultant at 4:00pm. This was something of a shock because people usually had to wait months to see a consultant. He, in turn, told me that I needed to have further investigations into my severe anaemia and scheduled this for two weeks later, on 14th November. Again, I was surprised at the speed at which everything was going. Such tests normally involve a three-month delay.

On the scheduled day of the appointment I felt so dizzy that I actually passed out. My GP then arranged for me to be admitted to hospital. I was so weak that I had to be transported in a wheelchair. I was subsequently admitted and given a blood transfusion. Then the doctors told me that I had cancer, which was a huge shock and the last thing that I was expecting.

I was devastated by what was happening to me. I had been ill for about eighteen months and just three weeks after the elders had prayed for me I was in hospital, having had a blood transfusion and now facing major surgery. God had healed my depression on one particular day. But the cancer would not be instantly cured.

In spite of everything, I was impressed by God's perfect timing. The very day that I was admitted to hospital was the same day that Jane started a new job there. Each morning she would turn up early to work so that she could visit me. Then she would come over in her lunch break and at the end of the day. She also cleaned our house and prepared meals for Michael and our youngest daughter, Lucy.

I was in hospital for two and a half weeks and was stunned by the support of local Christians and the entire Goldstone Church leadership team, who came out in force to pray for me. The cancerous tumour was in my colon, so this was removed, together with my gall bladder and two large stones. The following day I was sitting up feeling well and experiencing an amazing mixture of joy and peace. I had not responded well to my previous surgery so this was a welcome answer to prayer.

While the operation had been successful, the consultant informed me that the cancer had spread to my lymph glands. They removed nine lymph nodes, four of which had cancer. Eight days after the operation I came out of hospital and was surprised that other patients who'd had surgery a few days before me were still there.

At this time Lucy was struggling to believe that her father really cared about me as he seemed to show little emotion over my diagnosis. His police training demanded that 'you just deal with the situation in which you find yourself and you don't show your emotions'. Michael simply lived by this code. But one day Lucy saw him get into his police car in the driveway and put his head in his hands, obviously very upset and emotional. From that day on she saw him in a new way. Others also viewed him differently when, after my diagnosis, he got up and spoke to the church one Sunday morning and, with tears streaming down his face, told everyone that I had cancer and that it had spread. This was not the self-controlled Michael that he portrayed to the world.

Just before I left hospital, the consultant told me that I would need six months of chemotherapy. I should have been devastated, but inside I was feeling incredibly peaceful and full of praise to God for his answers to people's prayers. There was such a joy inside me. It was truly amazing, something I'll never forget. God knew what I needed in order to get through the next few months. When I arrived home, people from my church were incredibly kind. They cooked and brought meals round to the house for me and my family.

I may have had difficulties communicating in the past, but now I could not stop sharing my faith with others, telling them how wonderful God was and what he was doing in me. He challenged my poor sense of self-worth by inspiring over a hundred people to send me get well cards, and astounded me with the knowledge that Christians from around the UK and the USA were praying for me. I could hardly believe the care and concern expressed towards me. It was truly humbling.

While I was recovering from surgery I was handed a copy of the minutes from the last bookshop management meeting. I had not been told that there even was a meeting and I was very upset, feeling that I'd been written off because I had cancer. Depression was threatening to replace my joy and I was beginning to question my faith. Later God helped me to understand the reason for this reaction.

By now Lucy was attending Sunday meetings at the Christian Outreach Centre (later renamed City Coast Church) in Hove. She desperately wanted me to go to a healing service because she believed that if I attended I would be healed. I went because it was important to her, but my attitude was not great because I was still feeling that I'd been side-lined. However, while people were praying for me I had an overwhelming awareness of the Holy Spirit and an incredible sense of peace. I now see this experience as a time when God did something special in my emotions. This was particularly evidenced by my changed attitude to managing the shop. I stopped trying to control the situation and left the outcome in God's hands. I was happy to work or not, as he decided. Nevertheless, it was a hard choice to go to the Books Alive Christmas celebrations, although I was glad that I went.

The following day I turned up at the hospital ready for the first five days of six months' chemotherapy. I had been told that in order to keep as much of my hair as possible I should have it cut short and avoid perms and colours. I followed this advice. The initial treatment left me feeling cold, tired and very low. Christmas that year was a hard time of physical recovery.

God used the story of Mary and Martha to speak to me. One of the sisters was spiritual, the other practical. Back in 1991 my pastor was always telling me to be more of a Mary (ironically my name!) and not a Martha. I had always thought that Jesus was mistaken: Mary was the lazy one but Martha had it right. She was doing stuff and I was like her, always keen to serve others. Like a lot of busy 'Marthas' I did not realise that my self-worth lay in what I did.

I started to think about the two sisters, and what Jesus may have been going through by the time he reached their house. He was on his way to a terrible death in Jerusalem and was probably battling with the call of the cross. What he undoubtedly needed was an oasis of calm away from the demands of the crowds. Mary was sensitive to this, but Martha seemed more concerned about his receiving the best possible welcome, so she rushed around fussing and preparing. She was so preoccupied with her own agenda that she threatened to destroy the peace and quiet.

God forced me to sit at his feet. I was too ill to do anything but listen and I began to question my goals in life. Martha was too busy to be with Jesus and had missed the primary focus. What was my focus? Was I so busy with my family, job and community service that I had neglected what was most important? The Psalmist says, *'The one thing I ask of the Lord – the thing I seek most – is to live in the house of the Lord all the days of my life, delighting in the Lord's perfections and meditating in his Temple'* (Psalm 27:4 NLT).

I knew Wendy from church used to pray for others at the London Healing Mission and was a trained counsellor. She had previously told me that she waited for God to lead people to her for prayer. However, she felt prompted by the Holy Spirit to ask if she could pray for me, which she did every week for the next year.

When she first approached me, I thought, 'Well, cancer is serious enough for me to allow her to pray for me.' It was not a great reaction, but that's how I felt and responded at the time. God had already healed me from depression, so surely he could heal me from cancer too. I did not realise that there was so much more that he wanted to sort out in me than cancer. I was ignorant of the depth of his love for me and how much more needed to be changed in my life.

God taught me an incredible amount through that year with Wendy, but two things stood out: love and forgiveness. I thought that I knew God's love but when Wendy prayed for me I realised that I just needed to let him love me without my doing anything in return.

At the time I was not aware that I was entertaining any unforgiveness but as I thought about it, God brought someone to mind from the past. I had buried the memories but I knew that I had to forgive because God had forgiven me and because his Word told me to forgive. It wasn't easy, but after about three days I was finally prepared to let go. Initially, forgiveness was an act of will rather than feelings, but as soon as I released the offender something happened. God began showing me the reasons for their behaviour and gave me a deep compassion for them. This, as Wendy predicted, was another step towards my total healing.

I was back at work in January 1995, but not for long. Within a couple of weeks, I was feeling so tired that I realised I needed to pull out of running the bookshop until I had finished the chemotherapy treatment. I was concerned about the loss of income but God clearly told me to trust him for the finances so I obeyed him. I soon learnt that when you step out and trust God in an unfamiliar area (in this case, financial), more challenges arrive in that same area. The car failed its MOT and we faced an expensive bill. Then the gas man disconnected our boiler because he said that it was too dangerous. For a while we had no hot water and no heating – which was no fun in January.

Before each new session of chemotherapy, I had to have a blood test. Since my blood results were not quite right, I had to wait until 23rd

January before I could have my second five-day bout. That same week both my dad and his brother Harold, who lived with my parents, were taken into hospital. Dad had breathing problems and unfortunately Harold passed away on the Friday. A week later our daughter Jane was hospitalised too. The chemotherapy was making me very emotional and tearful, as was the realisation that Dad's life could be coming to an end (he actually lived for the next four years).

Everything seemed to be spiralling out of control, and the chemotherapy was having an adverse effect on me. To keep my spirits up I listened to lots of Christian cassette tapes and watched several Christian videos (DVDs hadn't been invented then). I was having to hand things over to God and trust him in a way that I had never done before.

My next chemotherapy session was due to begin in mid-February. I had a blood test on the Friday beforehand and learnt that my blood count level was so low that postponement seemed almost inevitable. Another test the following Monday would reveal if it had improved sufficiently for the third treatment to go ahead. This would require a big miracle so Wendy and I prayed together for it.

On the Sunday evening I went to the Church of Christ the King to hear John Arnott. I told a few people that I needed a miracle and they prayed for me. It was a marvellous evening. I did not leave the church building until 11:30pm because God was so powerfully at work, filling me with the Holy Spirit to the point that I almost felt drunk. The following day my blood count was far higher than it needed to be, so the next session of chemotherapy began. By the end of the week I had had so many injections that my veins were starting to give up. I asked people to pray about this and went around telling my friends how God had miraculously raised my blood count level a few days before.

More people prayed for me at the next Sunday evening service at CCK. Michael drove home so intoxicated by the Holy Spirit that he could not speak; he simply could not get the words out. We joked that if the police stopped us they would think that he was drunk on alcohol. I was on a high as well and when we arrived home Lucy and Simon could not believe their eyes. Two apparently tipsy parents were probably a great embarrassment to them! But God knew exactly what we needed. There were other occasions when Michael was so affected by the Holy Spirit that he was unable to speak. All of them were such wonderful experiences; so full of joy.

Something that puzzled me was the reaction of my daughter Jane, who always seemed upset when people prayed for me, until someone asked her what was wrong. Apparently, she had discovered from the hospital that my life expectancy was two years, even with the chemotherapy treatment. Every time anyone prayed for me she would have a mental picture of me in a coffin. She had kept these fears to herself for the past two months and they were eating away at her.

By the time I got through half of my chemotherapy treatments I was struggling with tiredness, illness and hair loss. My energy levels were almost non-existent and I discovered that I had a gluten intolerance, which did not help matters. Nevertheless, God continued to be faithful to us and we battled on together. Even the Macmillan nurse was surprised by the change in me and could see how God was keeping my spirits up.

Michael and I had booked the week-long Christian celebration Spring Harvest before the cancer had been diagnosed, and it was a physically difficult time for me. I was so weak that Michael had to push me around in a wheelchair. Also, at this time we heard that my youngest sister had just had her first baby. We were due to visit her on the way home but sadly the baby survived only ten hours and we were advised not to go. The effects of the chemotherapy were taking their toll on me emotionally, but this news was the final straw.

Knowing how vulnerable I was, Michael asked a Spring Harvest counsellor to speak to me. He prayed and then said, 'Is God saying anything to you?' 'I have a sense of death over me,' I replied. 'I sense the same,' he said. I told him about my baby sister Beryl's death thirty-five years earlier and he began praying that I would be released from the pain that I had experienced then. Sobs came from deep inside me and they just kept coming and coming. I had never cried over Beryl's death and God was setting me free from years of hurt and heartache.

Then he filled me with a tremendous deep peace. It was another very special moment.

In May I was approaching the end of my chemotherapy treatment when I saw the consultant in the clinical oncology department. He told me that I had Duke's C adenocarcinoma of the caecum, classed as an advanced bowel malignancy. I was informed that there was nothing to be gained by routine follow-up scans as the cancer would return to the main organs and there was no treatment available. Happily, I had some very positive friends who were encouraging me to hold on and trust in God. As a result, the joy that I had lost returned.

The chemotherapy ended in July. My hair started to grow and my friends and family gave me a surprise party for my fiftieth, my first ever birthday celebration. After all I had come through, this was a very special time, with numerous friends and family turning up to share the occasion with me. I was aware that there was a death sentence hanging over me. No one knew how long I would live, but I was determined to enjoy the time that I had left.

Jane was healed from various allergies at Stoneleigh Bible Week. She had suffered from these for twenty-two years and I was amazed at the change in her. When she gave her testimony in public, she said that there was a real struggle going on inside. Did she really want to be healed? What would be the implications if she said, 'Yes'? Like me, she was only too aware of the battle that rages in the mind.

I was encouraged by Romans 8:37: *'in all these things we are more than conquerors through him who loved us'*. Christians have challenges and difficulties, but *'in all these things'* we are told that we are overcomers. We have been energised by God's dynamic power and there is no reason why we should not face life with a courageous attitude. I reasoned that God was allowing me to engage in struggles so that I could emerge from them strengthened and refined, rejoicing not in what I could do but in what God could do in me.

It had become clear to me that the battle waged was for my mind. Throughout my childhood I had been taught that you achieve only what you put into life, so I had naturally become a driven person. God was using the cancer to reveal his amazing grace and permitting my struggles to deepen my trust in him. I was being challenged to draw on his spiritual power and to see the good in past difficulties, however bad they seemed at the time. Christians are not saved by grace to grow by sweat. They live by grace alone.

Photographs

Mary with her parents, 1945

Me as the eldest child with brother and sister, my parents and grandparents. 1952

Dad, Mary, Pat, Peter, John & Mum on Brighton seafront. 1954

Simon's Christening with family. 1971

Girls Brigade heading out for Church Parade. 1985

Celebrating my 60th birthday & our 40th wedding anniversary. 2005

The small church we joined after arriving in Australia. 2006

Australian Christmas day breakfast with the family. 2007

Michael & I in Australia. 2007

Mike and Lucy doing a hilarious sketch. 2008

Happy days with the Grandchildren. 2011

Laying of the slab for our new home Feb 2012

Before Michael was admitted to hospital. 2012

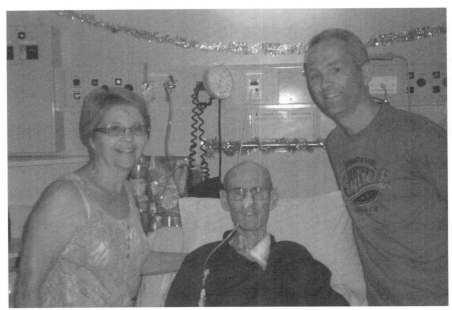

Simon and I visiting Michael. December 2012

Australian thanksgiving service for Michael. July 2013

Me with our children after Michael's death. December 2013

Me with our grandchildren after Michael's death. December 2013

The last of my home being packed into the container. 2014

The incredible church farewell cake. March 2014

Family celebrating my 70th birthday in UK. July 2015

Captains of Southwick Girls Brigade since 1983
at the 75th Anniversary. November 2017

Celebrating another UK birthday. July 2019

Chocolate happiness in Australia. December 2019

Another "Goodbye" with my girls. January 2020

Pressing On

Our second holiday to Kos was a vast improvement on our trip the previous year. No one needed to remind me how ghastly I had felt on the 1994 holiday. By sharp contrast, the second break was particularly refreshing. I was feeling well from the start and was determined to enjoy myself. On the second day my energy levels had depleted somewhat, so I relaxed on a sunbed and listened to cassette tapes on overcoming mental strongholds. The preacher explained that we can do all things through Christ who strengthens us (Philippians 4:13), that God is our strength and that we can overcome any obstacle if we trust him.

To test this teaching, I decided that despite the way I felt, I would swim from one island to another and back again (a fair distance), with Michael in a canoe beside me in case I got into difficulties. I accomplished the round trip without incident and felt more energetic at the end of my quest than when I had started. On my return I went for a two-hour sailing lesson and a long ride on a banana boat. I ended the day swimming multiple lengths of the swimming pool. Stepping out in faith seemed to be working and I was amazed at the strength that God gave me.

Not surprisingly, I was feeling rather stiff and tired the next day! But I was not ready to give in, so against Michael's advice I decided to go sailing on my own. He said that it was too windy, but my determination got the better of me. I sailed for a short time, capsized the boat, righted it, sailed on, then finally, with instruction from Michael and the rescue boatman, gave up because the wind was too strong for me.

The Sunday evening service was held at some old ruins on one of the beaches. It was a special time. The talk was from Matthew 5:9, *'Blessed are the peacemakers for they shall be called sons of God'* (NKJV). I had been reading about God's love in the morning and as I listened I suddenly became aware that I was enjoying a deeper sense of love and peace than I had ever known before.

At this time, God was speaking to me through several Bible verses. Romans 5:1–5 highlights faith, peace and hope, declaring that tribulations produce perseverance, perseverance character, and character hope. Then James 1:2–5 exhorts us to count it all joy when we fall into various trials as the testing of our faith produces patience. Psalm 100 was also challenging me about my attitudes. It was an exciting time, as if God was giving me personal lessons about himself and what he was doing in me.

Two months later I went to a conference at the Brighton Centre where the main speaker was John Wimber. I was sitting in a prominent raised section of the auditorium when, during a quiet moment, I was overcome by a wave of hilarity. I laughed helplessly, slid down my seat and ended up on the floor in a kind of glorious hysteria. So much for my usual reluctance to draw attention to myself! It was as if the tears in April and the release from grief at Spring Harvest were now giving way to incredible joy. It was an amazing experience.

In December a similar thing happened to Michael at a Signs and Wonders Conference in Olympia. We were praying in groups and he fell flat on his face and lay there for over an hour. When he eventually got up, he was totally bemused and could not speak for about thirty minutes. God was clearly doing a work in both of us after all the pain that we had been through.

When I arrived home, an advertisement in a local newspaper caught my attention. It was for computing classes for beginners. The world of computing was foreign to me. I did not know anything about keyboards or what a mouse was but I was suddenly struck by the desire to learn. This was a massive challenge for me because of my lack of education and I feared that others would discover how terrible my spelling and English were. But, surprisingly undaunted, I signed up for the twenty-week course.

Although it was advertised as a beginners' course, I soon discovered that most of those who attended had some knowledge of computing. It seemed that the teacher was prepared to help those who were making progress but left me out. Also, others were able to practise on their home computers, but since I did not have one, I was at a big disadvantage and lagged far behind the rest. Finally, I mustered up a lot of courage and complained to the class organiser, who dealt with my complaint very sympathetically. The following week I received a little more help. I also bought a cheap second-hand computer so that I could get some practice. I never dreamt then that one day my skills would have improved so much that I would be able to document my journey in writing. With my meagre aptitude for English, dyslexia and poor typing ability, this book is nothing short of miraculous.

Michael and I attended a Christian conference in Bournemouth but on the final day I was in agony. People prayed for me but the pain was a 'ten out of ten', so bad that I almost stopped at Chichester Hospital on the way home. However, I managed to see my doctor first and she phoned the hospital to say that I was on my way. I was admitted and my name was added to the church prayer chain. In the past I would have relied solely on the doctors, who, along with family and friends, thought that the cancer had returned. But my faith was growing and I sensed that the answer was prayer. Various tests such as scans and X-rays revealed that my white blood cells were fighting an infection. After ten days the pain had subsided and I was home.

At a church service the speaker was talking about the influences of the occult on individuals and I recognised some of those influences in me. I spoke to him and we prayed through the incidents that God highlighted. The next morning, I was back to my old self and within a couple of days I was feeling better than I had for over two years. A few days later Christian friends prayed again, sealing my deliverance.

In April, as the weather started to change, I was able to spend a lot of time tending to the garden, which was severely overgrown. As I worked I sensed God speaking to me about what he had done in my life. In one spot the weeds were so thick that they had totally covered the plants – one lovely white flower in particular. At times I had felt that there was so much rubbish in my life that no one (including me) could see the beauty underneath.

Once the weeds were cleared I noticed the stones that had come to the surface because of the winter storms. Through this God showed me how the storms of my life had unpleasant consequences and how he had been clearing them out. Stone-clearing was followed by pruning and I considered how some plants needed more ruthless pruning than others. Again, there are times in our lives when we need more pruning. Some plants grow at a rapid rate after pruning while others grow at a slower pace. In the same way we all grow at different rates. It intrigued and frustrated me that the weeds refused to stay inactive! They kept coming back fast. This reminded me that once an area of our lives has been cleared, other things start to surface, often emerging with different leaf types and colour. The devil often makes it hard to discern the legitimate from the counterfeit.

Sonia was an old school friend of mine who emigrated to Canada in 1963. Over the years we had both become Christians and had continued to write to each other, which was the way you communicated in 1996. She and her American husband Tom were now living in Seattle. Recalling that my life expectancy was two years, I did not think I had much time left on earth and one thing on my bucket list before I died was to visit them, as neither Michael nor I had been to America or met Tom. So, Michael and I flew to Seattle in August 1996.

Tom and Sonia introduced us to Marriage Ministries International (MMI). They were leaders in this organisation, teaching God's way in marriage. While we were staying with them they were teaching on a training weekend, during which couples were being equipped to teach others about marriage. Michael and I were invited to attend the weekend.

In April 1997 we were also invited to attend the MMI International Conference in Denver, where we received additional training. This was another big step in our spiritual growth. We both gained an enormous amount from the teaching and made some wonderful friends who had a greater spiritual depth than we knew at the time.

By 1999, we were thoroughly involved with MMI. Not only was God equipping us to help others with their marriages; he was enhancing ours too. God taught us that our lives and marriages were like icebergs: 90% unseen and 10% revealed. As the sun shines, it melts the top of the iceberg and exposes what needs to be dealt with and transformed. The central issue is love, which means not pursuing selfish desires and abandoning the relationship when those desires remain unmet. We choose to love because God loves us unconditionally. He promised the land of Canaan to the Israelites, but they needed to inherit it little by little. We have been given the Holy Spirit so that we can gradually press into our promised land – whatever that 'land' may be for each of us.

I had a picture of a pathway full of high weeds and brambles which made progress very difficult. I then sensed the Lord say that he would clear a pathway for us and he did just that.

At another MMI conference in Denver, I discovered that fear was part of pride, because it took the focus off the Lord and onto the individual. Suddenly I realised that I was full of fear. It was a breakthrough moment then. But even as I addressed it, I still had to battle with fear from time to time.

I was struggling with poor health and lacked energy to do much, so it was helpful when God gave me another encouraging picture. I saw cooked mince, like a Bolognaise sauce being poured onto a plate. There was no end to the flow, the sauce just kept coming and coming. God seemed to be promising me, 'I will supply ALL your needs.' He was true to his word as this was an important picture for us in the years that lay ahead. It is important to keep hold of prophetic words or pictures as they can be a great source of encouragement.

Michael retired from work as a policeman in August 1999 and took a civilian job in the Sussex Police Photographic Department. By 2000 we had been working with MMI for three years, running courses in the UK to promote good marriages. We did not realise then that this ministry marked the start of a change in direction for us both.

Michael and I were planning a holiday before our visit to another training conference in Denver, but the flights were expensive so we abandoned the idea. In hindsight it seemed that God stopped us so that we could spend more time with a couple called Jack and Pam, who unexpectedly invited us to stay with them after the Denver conference.

We had never been to any of their church services before but attended a midweek meeting with them. To our astonishment the pastor, Lorie Hagen, a stranger to us, called us out to the front and began prophesying over us – a scary experience when we did not know anyone present. This is what he said to us:

> 'The first time I saw you, man and woman of God, I saw that you were called for such a time as this. God has watched your walk. Get ready. Now is the time of transition. I have prepared you a new habitation. The next dimension of your ministry will be in power and authority. It has been a slow process. You have asked why and how. You will be in the cave no more, no more obscure. I have anointed your eyes with an eye salve to give you new understanding, man of God. You will operate in a new understanding, divine wisdom in a new dimension and in a new direction. I release in you a prophetic ministry. You will walk now having a flow of words of knowledge and words of wisdom. I have given you an understanding and a divine endowment to know the mysteries and discern the carnal from the kingdom of the Most High. You will take the word to them that God will not deliver them out of their circumstances but will take them through. Daughter of Zion, there is healing in your hands. This will go with you wherever you go. You will carry it with you and you will impart and walk in my authority. You will now do it through me.'

God started to speak to me from Judges. Gideon was an insignificant man who God found hiding in a winepress and called him (Judges 6:11–16). He discovered that he was important not because of his notable abilities or desires, (verse 15), but because God had a purpose for him. He trusted God's call and followed his strategy to overcome the Midianites (Judges 7:1–22). In the same way, we find true significance only when we trust and obey God's call and stick to his divine plan. I felt like Gideon – very ordinary with no notable abilities – but I did trust God and wanted to obey him.

In January 2001 I was still physically weak, so it was a tremendous encouragement when my pastor gave me a word from God: 'I will bring health and healing to it (Mary); I will heal my people (Mary) and will let them (Mary) enjoy abundant peace and security' (see Jeremiah 33:6). He told me that God wanted me to substitute my name for that of God's people. I took his words to heart and began praying that they would be true for me. Instinctively, I sensed that God was going to bring me through the physical weakness brought on by the chemotherapy.

Several scriptures spoke to me in early 2001. It struck me that some of the Israelites preferred not to enter the Promised Land that God had prepared for them (Numbers 32). This made me consider whether we are prepared to settle for less than God's best. Surely, we need to press in and lay hands on all that he has for us.

Then in Deuteronomy 4, I read about Moses' exhortation to Israel to obey God. The whole of the land of Canaan lay open to the Israelites and Moses warned them not to add to or take away from what God had said. He then gave them the secret of wisdom in life: observing and obeying the word of God. To access God's blessing all that they needed to do was obey. Our Canaan opens up for us when we do as he says. I read on in Deuteronomy and noted that God tests us to humble us and reveal what's really in our hearts (Deuteronomy 8:1–5). He brought his people out of Egypt on the back of miracles and can do the same for us, but we need to trust him in the difficult times.

I suddenly realised that living independently from God is the root of all sin and that the way to overcome sin and temptation is to live by the Spirit. That means totally trusting God in everything. It's only when we walk in the knowledge we have that God gives us more. Sure, we will make mistakes, but we will be wiser for them. Our job is simply to trust and obey him. He knows our heart.

In April 2001 I started praying the prayer of Jabez from 1 Chronicles 4:10 *'Jabez cried out to the God of Israel, "Oh, that you would bless me and enlarge my territory! Let your hand be with me, and keep me from harm so that I will be free from pain." And God granted his request.'* I had no idea then how greatly we would be blessed and our territory enlarged.

Australia

It was August 2001. I was at a church picnic in the park when, in the course of conversation, someone encouraged me to read a book called *No Well-Worn Paths* by Terry Virgo. I did not expect it to change our lives the way it did.

As I read, I sensed that God was saying two things to me: 'Join the Church of Christ the King (CCK) in Brighton' (now renamed Emmanuel) and 'Go and help plant a church in Australia'. Both of these would take us way out of our comfort zones. For a start, we preferred small churches and CCK (Emmanuel Church) had about 900 members at that time. Additionally, the thought of retiring to the other side of the world did not sit easily for someone who had always lived within a fifty-mile radius of Brighton. I kept these seemingly crazy ideas to myself for a long time because I reasoned that if they were from God, he would speak independently to Michael about them. It was not my job to persuade him on either count, so I just prayed and I also asked God where in that vast country he would like us to settle down. I knew something about Sydney, but when the word, 'Perth' came straight to my mind, I was somewhat curious.

About two months later, we attended our grandson's dedication at CCK (Emmanuel Church) and God clearly spoke to Michael about changing churches. He noticed how the men were participating in more dynamic ways than in the fellowship that we were attending. He could hear the men singing in worship; they also prayed out and gave words of prophecy. He was the sort of person who never hesitated when he heard from God, so the following day he spoke to our pastor and by the end of the week we had a new spiritual home. The rapid transition was hard at first. As a newcomer, I looked around at the large numbers of people and felt very much out of my comfort zone.

As we took steps to become members of CCK, Michael began asking about training courses that the church ran. I was very surprised by this because it was not something that we had talked about. Evidently, God was starting to stir something deep in my husband's heart. We became members in early 2002.

Things changed at a rapid rate. By September Michael had given up his job in the Fingerprint Bureau at Sussex Police and we had enrolled on a year-long training course with the church. This course was open to all ages but was primarily directed towards young people who wanted to spend a year serving God (often between school and university). However, when we told the elders that God seemed to be leading us in this direction, we were happily accepted onto the course.

Michael was more at ease with the course than me. I found it very frightening. God appeared to be pushing me into unfamiliar territory in every area of my life. My health was still an issue and some days I just had to relax and trust God, which was particularly important once we realised that our outgoings exceeded our income. God was totally faithful in this, always ensuring that we had enough money to pay our bills, satisfy our needs and give us the stamina that we required to complete the course. I was amazed at his provision. We did not have any extra money but we did not go into debt; it was a total mystery. At the end of the year the church offered us both jobs. Michael's was full time, mine was part-time.

In November 2003 we returned to the USA for a holiday. First, we visited our friends Tom and Sonia in Seattle and travelled with them to Vancouver to visit Sonia's parents, whom I had known as a child before they had emigrated to Canada. Michael and I then went on to San Diego where we were bowled over by the Remembrance Day Parade, which differed considerably from its counterpart in the UK. We agreed that our visits to the States were not just holidays but times when we met some wonderful Christians, who had a significant impact on our growth in faith.

During this period in my life, several people gave me encouraging words that they believed were from God. Here are some of them:

'You're like Tinkerbell in Peter Pan. As you float about you'll leave gold dust everywhere and the dust will fall on everyone you touch.'

'I can see a picture of a jug half empty or half full, being transparent with a beautiful rose in it:

1. God is restoring what the locust has taken.
2. God will give back in abundance.
3. Continue to be transparent, don't let others close you down.
4. You are a beautiful rose.'

(I was likened to a rose again in 2016, see chapter 11).

'The thief comes only to steal and kill and destroy; I have come that they may have life, and have it to the full.' (John 10:10)

'God will use you to bless others simply by the person that you are.'

'God has more for you to come.'

These words were very inspiring because they did not reflect the way that I saw myself. I think that God wanted to encourage me because he knew I didn't feel that I had anything to offer. I was simply someone heading towards my retirement years.

In August 2004, nearly ten years after my cancer treatment, I was still struggling with poor health. For this reason, Michael and I tried to have cheap holidays in the sun in February and October. The warmth and relaxation helped to keep me going. Then we spent a family weekend at my sister's house in Lincoln, with both my brothers and their wives, my sisters and their husbands, and Mum. My family, who had not seen me for a while, were unaware of my continuing health struggles and were concerned when they saw me spending so much time on the sun lounger simply because I did not have the energy to do much more than that.

Six months after that break I was talking to a couple who said that God had spoken to them about going to live in Australia. 'Where in Australia?' I had asked him. 'Perth,' he had replied. At this point I had not told anyone what I believed God had said to me. Immediately, I identified with this and my excitement knew no bounds.

Michael and I were planning a special holiday to celebrate our fortieth wedding anniversary and my sixtieth birthday, but we could not agree on the destination. I had wanted to visit Australia since I was eighteen years old but Michael was not interested. When he was in the Navy, he had visited Fremantle in Australia decades before. He usually decided where we went away and I was happy to let him lead on this – so long as it did not cost much and the weather was hot. This holiday, however, was different because it was a special celebration. That thought prompted Michael to begin secretly looking at the possibility of a trip to the other side of the world.

I got my dream holiday in April 2005. We spent five wonderful weeks in Australia, starting in Adelaide and visiting Kangaroo Island, then staying in Sydney with friends we had met in America, who were the National Directors in Australia for Marriage Ministries International. Then we drove up the east coast to Brisbane, visited more friends from MMI, and finally flew to Cairns to stay with friends from CCK (Emmanuel). While we were in Cairns we spent time exploring the outback in the middle of nowhere.

One morning Michael got up early to watch the wildlife. This was when God spoke to him about moving to Australia. As soon as we arrived home he started investigating the immigration process and discovered that we needed a 410 self-funding retirement visa. We should have acted immediately but delayed our application. This delay threw all our plans into jeopardy because a few weeks later Michael discovered that the 410 visa was being withdrawn on 30th June, just one week away.

It was June 24th when I read Ephesians 5:22: 'Wives, submit to your own husbands, as to the Lord' (NKJV). This verse suddenly spoke to me in a different way. I believed that my submission to Michael and to the Lord had progressed, but I had never connected the two together until now. I sensed that I should not go racing ahead, but that we should communicate and I should then let him make the next decision.

Both agencies that we contacted informed us that we did not have enough time to apply for or receive the relevant amount of pension needed for the visa, so I just prayed and the word 'APPLY' kept going around in my head. Michael's response was, 'Let's apply and see what happens.' So I lined up the paperwork across our living room floor and worked through it methodically. As I started filling in the forms I realised that when we sold our house (now mortgage-free), we could put the proceeds in the bank as cash, which would earn interest. This interest would then make up the shortfall on the pension side.

We were notified that it would take three months to obtain the deeds of the house, but when I explained the situation, we actually received them in three days. Against all the odds I was able to post everything off by special delivery within the week to arrive the day before the deadline. God is so faithful when we trust him and do as he says.

'Surely God gives us common sense' – these words kept going around in my mind after a well-meaning friend kept repeating them to me. Common sense told me to go to Perth before we decided to live there. What if we didn't like the place? I kept these concerns to myself rather than sharing them with Michael. Then God spoke to me from Hebrews 11:8: 'It was by faith that Abraham obeyed when God called him to leave home and go to another land' (NLT). God knew my anxious thoughts – that was both encouraging and faith-building.

Joshua 1:8–9 encouraged me too: 'Study this Book of Instruction continually. Meditate on it day and night so you will be sure to obey everything written in it. Only then will you prosper and succeed in all you do. This is my command – be strong and courageous! Do not be afraid or discouraged. For the Lord your God is with you wherever you go.' (NLT).

Once the emigration department had notified us of the receipt of our application, we went ahead with the required police checks and medicals. Only after this could we put our house up for sale. The UK housing market was static at the time, but not for us! Our sale was completed in two months and our belongings were shipped out within five months of our visa application. Indeed, the process was so fast that we actually had to stay with friends for ten weeks before we left for far-off shores.

Immediately after we had sold the house I began wondering about buying a small flat in the UK as an insurance policy in case things did not work out. It was then I was reading about Lot's wife (Genesis

19:26; Luke 17:32) and was persuaded not to. She looked back and became a pillar of salt. God clearly indicated to us that we had been called to trust him for the future and not to insure ourselves against failure. Interestingly, the financial crash happened about three years later in the UK but not in Australia.

We arrived in Perth on 18ᵗʰ January 2006 and within three weeks we had found a house that was double the size and half the price of the one we had sold in the UK. At the beginning of March, just five weeks later, we moved into our new home in Beeliar, about twenty miles south of Perth, and became members of a small church group known as Wellspring. Michael quickly joined the leadership team but I had no official role at this time. I sensed God saying 'just be', so I focused on getting to know him better by reading and studying his Word. The earlier words about being strong and courageous and not being afraid or discouraged helped me to focus on the fact that God had a purpose for us in Australia.

One thing that surprised me was my reaction to being away from all my family and friends in England. I had expected to be dreadfully homesick, but I was totally content with our new life. God was obviously at work in me and during the first few months in our new surroundings I reflected on the amazing way that he had blessed me and given me joy when I had not known what real joy was. He had been:

> My **healer** – mentally (from rejection, depression, sadness and hurts) and also physically;
>
> My **friend** – always available and reliable, someone who never let me down;
>
> My **shield** – against the devil and all the fiery arrows that came against me;
>
> My **strength** – both physically and mentally, giving me the ability to overcome challenges;
>
> My **peace** – changing a constant worrier into someone who trusted him implicitly;

My **guide** – in life, in finding a new home, in relationships;

My **comforter** – when things didn't go the way I wanted or expected;

My **protector** – from accidents at home or in the car.

Shortly after we arrived in Perth Michael began working as a volunteer for two rescue organisations: The State Emergency Service (SES) and the Bush Fire Brigade (BFB). Members of the SES were particularly busy when the winter storms hit and the BFB had their work cut out fighting bush fires in the summer. Michael used to joke about needing to remember which uniform to put on. The SES clothing was bright orange, while the BFB was lime yellow with a white helmet. I often told him that he had no dress sense at all!

Just a year after we had moved to Australia we had a lovely surprise. Our daughter Lucy came to live with us on a study visa while she studied and worked. After two years she was able to get a visa to stay, found a full-time job and moved in with friends.

Two months later there was another surprise when our other daughter Jane and her family came to stay with us. They had visas to live permanently 'down under' and immediately started looking for a home. They found one with a swimming pool, which was great for the boys who were learning to swim. Our son-in-law, a nurse, was soon able to start work in the local hospital. God had answered my prayer to live in Australia, but I certainly never imagined that he would call both of our daughters to live there as well.

A few years before arriving in Australia, I had been praying the prayer of Jabez: '"Oh, that you would bless me and enlarge my territory! Let your hand be with me, and keep me from harm, so that I will be free from pain." And God granted his request' (1 Chronicles 4:10).

Suzanne, the daughter of friends in the UK, came to live in Australia on a study visa and asked if she could stay with us for a couple of weeks until she found somewhere to live. That fortnight turned into six months, but she was a very easy guest and had the same sense of humour as Michael, so we had lots of fun and laughter together.

I was reminded of the word from Isaiah that someone had had for me: *'Enlarge your house; build on additions; spread out your home! For you will soon be bursting at the seams!'* (Isaiah 54:2-3 TLB). It seemed like a nice word, but little did we know then just how many visitors we would entertain in the following six years. At times we really were bursting at the seams. For the next four years we accustomed ourselves to our new life and entertained numerous family members and friends. We were also seen as the 'local hotel' for visitors to the church. We enjoyed getting to know our guests and Michael became an excellent tour guide and resident funny man.

We loved the outdoors and the somewhat unfamiliar traditions. Instead of the usual English Carol Service we had Carols in the Park. This event was not always organised by the churches so sometimes it did not reflect the heart of Christmas, but was more of a summer fair, with secular Christmas songs thrown in. However, our church did join with other churches to run Carols in the Park with a greater Christian emphasis. On Christmas Day we would go to the beach to cool down and watch the sun set over the sea. Australia Day, in January, is a public holiday, with picnics on the shore or in the parks followed by firework displays. Then in March we had church camps with water slides, cricket matches, barbecues and flying foxes (sliding down a zip wire). These events were all such fun.

In 2010, at my annual health check-up, the doctor looked at my records and said, 'Mmm… fifteen years. I think you've made it.' I suddenly realised that it was fifteen years since I had been told that I would live for a maximum of two years and probably only six months. It had been a very hard journey with lots of struggles, a journey of faith and trusting God to guide me – whether I lived or died. I did not go around thinking much about the initial prognosis, but the doctor's comment somehow lifted the death sentence and made me realise the impact that words can have on people.

I had never realised how much my parents had influenced me by their example. They brought me up to persevere, regardless of the odds against me. If I was determined enough, I believed I could do anything. That was both a positive attribute and a negative one.

During my years of depression, I had developed a way of coping with difficulties: to look inwards and work things out for myself – with disappointing results. Now that I had been healed of depression for a number of years I was discovering that old habits die hard. My first reaction to any difficulty was to deal with it myself rather than go straight to prayer. I still needed to learn and improve.

Bill Johnson was the main speaker at a conference that we attended in March 2011. It was memorable for all the wrong reasons, although it began well: my eyesight improved considerably when people prayed for my cataracts. On the third day I was enjoying a superb time of worship when waves of stomach pains hit me with increasing intensity. I felt as though I was in labour. By the end of the worship time I was feeling so ill that I decided to move to the back. I got as far as the door where I reasoned that I would either have to sit down or fall down. The next thing I knew I was on the floor with ambulance men staring down at me and then transporting me to Fremantle Hospital where a lot of wires were attached to me. Strangely, all the tests came back normal, but since I was left completely washed out, I did not return to the conference and instead spent a few days recovering. I never understood the experience, but decided to focus on the healing that God had already accomplished.

Later that month our son Simon, his wife and their two daughters (aged five and seven) visited us for the first time. Actually, Eloise celebrated her eighth birthday with an Australian-style barbecue on the beach. To give them a better understanding of the country, we took them away for a few days' break. Michael and I stayed in our caravan while they slept in a tent that we had borrowed for them. One memory that the girls won't forget happened during one of our barbecues together. A kookaburra, which was sitting in a tree about ten metres away, suddenly swooped down and snatched a sausage from one of their plates. Kookaburras are renowned for their laughter and this one did not disappoint. It was as though he was sitting in the tree giggling at us.

A friend of mine kindly took some photos of us all together: Lucy, Jane and her family and Simon and his family. These photos were burned onto discs, one for each family. I did not realise how significant this was at the time. These pictures would be the last ones that we would have of all of us together.

It was a great adventure. We had now lived in Perth for five and a half years, during which time we had returned to the UK on three occasions to see family and friends. In Australia we had enjoyed visits to Sydney and Cairns in Queensland and travelled up and down the western coast. Australia is the sixth-largest country in the world and the entire country is larger than the whole of Europe. A completely new world had opened up to us in our retirement years.

Life there was anything but dull. There were hours of sunshine, but floods and bushfires too. While we were in Queensland heavy rain caused the riverbanks to overflow and flood houses to rooftop level. Consequently, the rivers were very fast flowing and quite frightening, but they ensured that the waterfalls in the area were totally spectacular. In sharp contrast, we arrived back in Perth to bone-dry conditions and dams with dangerously low water levels. We were informed that if we did not have rain soon there wouldn't be enough water to see Perth through the year.

After Lucy moved out I had begun using her bedroom as my scrapbooking room. This pleased Michael, who often complained that my hobby was taking over the room that we both used. The problem was that my new venue was further down the hallway and I began to feel isolated there and missed my husband's company. So one day I decided to move back.

Any scrap-booker will know what this entails in the way of moving equipment and materials, as well as the furniture in which to store them. I had to empty the storage units of heaps of stuff, transport them down the corridor and fill them up again at the other end. This momentous activity was scheduled for the time when Michael was at his SES training evening. I slipped a bed sheet under the units and dragged them, one by one, along the tiled corridor and round the corners. By the time Michael got home all the furniture had been moved but there was stuff all over the place. He could not believe that I had managed to fit the units into 'his' room and I needed to exercise a little female charm to persuade him that this was a good idea, as I was lonely without him.

Michael and I had become used to temperatures of 35°C to 40°C. But from June to September the temperature in the Perth area drops to a very cold 18°C to 20°C. Exmouth, some 2,000 miles north of Perth, is where the 'grey nomads' and lots of retirees go for the sun and heat at this time of the year. It made complete sense for us to join up with some friends and, caravans in tow, head north for a big adventure together. After three days' travelling and 2,000 miles behind us, we arrived in Exmouth and were joined by a host of other holidaymakers who ranged from backpackers to those with palaces on wheels.

We visited the Cape Range National Park, which runs down the coastline of the Ningaloo Marine Park, now a world heritage protected area. Some of the best beaches in Western Australia are located there and the turquoise water fulfils the longings of any keen snorkeler. The Jurabi Coastal Reserve and Turtle Centre is situated in an area of white beaches with scattered reefs. This is where the turtles come each year to lay their eggs. To swim and snorkel in such incredible conditions was beyond our wildest dreams. It goes without saying that we had the most superb holiday and felt very privileged to have been there.

The last family photo before Mike died
Simon and his family, Mike and I, Lucy and Jane and her family,
March 2011

Coming Back

In September 2011 the recession in the UK had a dramatic effect on the exchange rate and on our income as a result, so Michael and I decided that it would be wise to cut our expenses by looking for a smaller and cheaper house. We saw dozens of show homes and were stunned by the facilities on offer. The standard Australian size seemed to incorporate four bedrooms, two bathrooms, a games room, study, laundry room, outdoor entertaining area, barbecue and swimming pool.

We were looking for something more modest and soon discovered that the cheapest option was to buy a plot of land and build our own property. We eventually decided on a three-bedroom, two-bathroom plan and put our house on the market at the beginning of September. Much to our amazement, within six weeks we had completed the sale on our home, put our possessions in storage and moved out.

By this time Jane was living in a property that was situated on about half an acre of land, so we parked our caravan in her back yard and lived between that and a bedroom and lounge in her house. Work on our new home in Baldivis, about seventy minutes' drive south of Perth, started on 17th February. UK builders dig foundations but in Australia they lay a sand foundation first, add a concrete base on that, then build the house on top of both. The reason for this is simple: in the event of an earthquake, the whole house will move and it will be less likely to collapse.

Of some amusement to Michael was my scrapbooking hobby, which was my way to record our family history for our children and grandchildren. Michael, however, was soon declaring that my numerous scrapbooking albums and materials were going to require some seriously strong foundations in our new home!

About this time God gave someone a word for me, likening me to a crystal water-lily in a sparkling pool:

As the Son/sun shone warmly and gently down on the lily, so God was smiling because he was pleased with me.

The lily was open to him in every direction. Wherever I served, I delighted to face towards him.

The lily had been crafted by the Father, carefully and delicately sculptured, honed. God had worked his beauty into me.

Just as he'd fashioned the lily flowers, so I had allowed God to refine the gifts that I had offered him.

Crystal is clear and I had no hidden motives, but was open to everyone.

While a real water lily is easily crushed, a crystal one is strong. When hit it makes a ringing sound and God had made me strong.

The pool was full of water, a reminder that the Holy Spirit was filling me with life, upholding me and keeping me cool and steady.

A lily just sits on water and God was sparkling with joy at my restful trust in him.

Just as the water surrounds a lily, so God was preventing evil from reaching, breaking or damaging me. It was a picture of being, not doing.

The slightest move of a lily sent ripples across the pool and in the same way I was affecting and delighting others.

The stem of the lily was attached to the roots and I was planted firmly in Jesus.

The sap/life under the lily was yellow. It cascaded through the crystal petals and sparkled on them like small fibre optics. The yellow colour expressed joy, which moved out from me to bless others.

There were also other colours in the crystal flowers and God's blessings were flowing through me.

The pond was pale blue-green and symbolised holiness and life.

The overall picture was one of order, symmetry, trust, peacefulness and tranquillity, yet it had life, colour and movement.

This word greatly encouraged me because it told me that God saw my heart and knew what was on the inside, what others could not see. It also confirmed to me what God was saying to me about being and not just doing. It is so easy to fall into the trap of consistently living to fulfil needs and feeling lazy about sitting down and drawing close to him. This idea would have even more significance over the coming months.

Good Friday was on 4th April. Michael and I joined some friends for a bike ride around Swan River and then enjoyed a barbecue with them. On 22nd he preached to our church. He would always ask my opinion after he had preached and, on this occasion, he spoke so well that I told him that he could not have done better. Looking back, it was as though God had enabled him to finish at his best. Although we did not know this at the time, this would be his last sermon and we would never cycle together again.

We collected the keys to our new home on 22nd June and, with the help of Lucy and one of her friends, started to decorate the whole of the inside with three coats of paint. It was a huge task. Australian homes are far bigger than UK homes and demand much more by way of painting. Michael began to struggle with intense tiredness and attributed it to the hard work involved. However, he was also eating very little, which was unusual for someone who normally had an extremely healthy appetite and loved his food. He told me that he simply did not feel hungry. In the end I persuaded him to visit the doctor, who gave him medication for reflux.

We moved into our new home on 9th July. By this time Michael was barely eating anything at all, although he claimed that he was OK. I was not convinced so I insisted on another visit to the doctor and went with him to ensure that he gave an accurate account of his symptoms. True to form, he tried to underplay the truth and I had to interject and enlighten the doctor that he was hardly eating anything now.

The doctor immediately sent us to the hospital emergency department. Michael was so laid back about it all that he demanded we stop off at our daughter's house to get a haircut on the way. A flu epidemic was in full swing and since children had first priority, we reckoned that we were in for a long wait in A&E. So serious was the flu problem that everyone was being told there were no spare beds available. Michael kept saying it was all a waste of time and I had to force him to wait.

Two hours later he was admitted, given an endoscopy and told that he had cancer of the oesophagus. Surprisingly, he was not at all fazed about the diagnosis but remained very positive and matter-of-fact about it. In light of my own healing I had no problem trusting God for the next step, although the girls were very shocked, particularly when it came to Michael's laid-back attitude.

In August, Michael returned to hospital for another endoscopy to check his oesophagus and to have keyhole surgery around his stomach. The cancer appeared to have been contained but we needed to wait for the biopsy results. There followed numerous trips to the hospital for blood tests and nine weeks of chemotherapy to reduce the tumour before an operation to remove it. At this stage Michael had to be fed every three hours through a tube that the doctors had inserted to bypass the tumour. Needless to say, he was too weak to do much around the house so our church elders and friends came to the rescue, putting up curtain rails and assembling a shed in the garden.

November was a challenging month but God often filled me with joy as I drove Michael to and from the hospital. One of the elders' wives shared with me a picture of large stones with water spurting out from among them. It was an illustration of how I was feeling; God's joy welling up in my heart as we drove back and forth down country roads through beautiful bushland. I would often tell Michael how happy I was that God had brought us to Australia. God was giving me the joy to help me cope with what was to come.

Our son, Simon, arrived from the UK to see his father and to support me while Michael went through surgery. Simon took over the driving, which was a relief and took some of the pressure off me. He and Michael were also able to enjoy some father-son bonding time, walking in the warm water of the Indian Ocean before his surgery.

The operation lasted seven and a half hours. The surgeon removed a section of Michael's oesophagus and then repositioned his stomach higher up. I saw him in intensive care and was somewhat alarmed at the number of tubes coming out of him. But three days later, with stubborn determination, Michael was walking to the lift to see me off, tubes still connected to an array of medical equipment on the trolley that he was pushing around.

Several people made long-distance visits to see Michael in hospital, notably Iain, a childhood friend of Simon's, who flew over from Sydney, and Fred and Heather who came from Queensland. Both flights lasted five hours. I started to realise how special Michael was to others and the impact he had made on them.

When he returned home he was on a liquid diet for two weeks and then on puréed foods. We hoped the biopsy results would confirm that the cancer had all been removed but were concerned when we were told that there was still some left. He went through a further nine weeks of chemotherapy and daily radiotherapy.

In January 2013 several friends visited from the UK. I was amazed at their concern for Michael and so thankful for their support. While I looked after him they helped in the kitchen and did jobs that Michael had not been able to do since we had moved into our new home, like putting up fixtures in the garage. Michael could no longer do practical things because the treatment was taking too much out of him. I was now responsible for the time-consuming task of making special nutritious foods, liquidising them and feeding them to him through a tube in his stomach every three hours. I battled to bolster his immune system with as many nutrients as I could, bearing in mind how much he could eat at any given time. In spite of all my efforts, his weight dropped to fifty-two kilos. Happily, in the middle of all this, we found time to paddle in the Indian Ocean together, which was a very therapeutic distraction.

We lived one day at a time and began using buses and trains to go to the hospital. It was relaxing travelling this way; just hanging out together, thanking God for forty-seven years of marriage and praying for more years to come. Looking back, it was a special time and I'm so grateful that we made the most of it.

Our friends continued to support us in all sorts of practical ways. One Sunday the church put together a work party and most of the members turned up to help. It was about 30°C outside and the majority wore essential sun hats. Gardens in the Perth area were just comprised of sand, so they laid a much-needed reticulation system (a piped water network for automatic watering) in our back yard. They also prepared the ground for a new lawn and laid concrete slabs. Then they put on a barbecue in the local park. Combining practical and social activities made this a fun-filled occasion, as did our frequent visits to the burger van after church services. Those friends were such a blessing to us. I am still amazed at their kindness.

Perth had been God's original destination for Michael and me and our goal was to help establish a church there. The first two elders were appointed in April, so we were now officially a church and Michael and I had essentially fulfilled our mission. 'What's next?' I wondered and began praying about it. At the time I assumed that life would go on much the same as before. I was wrong.

On 1st May Michael saw the oncologist, who spent some time scrolling up and down on his computer screen, noting the results of the latest scan. Finally, he told us that Michael still had the cancer and would need some more chemotherapy in three weeks' time. He said that Michael could still travel to the UK for my mother's ninetieth birthday celebrations and that if he needed further treatment while we were away, he could receive it in the UK. My reaction was somewhat matter-of-fact because I kept thinking that his healing was up to God, not the doctors. If God had healed me of terminal cancer, surely he would do the same for Michael, whose cancer had not (as far as I was aware) been officially labelled 'terminal'. Indeed, the medics had always acted as though he would be cured and I didn't doubt them.

In spite of the special assistance around the airports, our journey to the UK was not easy. Michael struggled to eat anything and was grateful for the soup that the staff produced from the first-class cabin. After a gruelling twenty-one hours, we arrived at Gatwick Airport, where we were met by my sister and her husband. Unbeknown to me, her first words to Michael were, 'How on earth did you make it?' To this he replied, 'Sheer willpower.' I had no idea how sick Michael was. I just was not accepting (or did not want to accept) what everyone else could clearly see.

We joined the congregation at CCK (Emmanuel Church) in Brighton on our first Sunday back in the UK and were overwhelmed by the welcome we received. During the offering, a large number of friends gathered around Michael to pray for him. I was impressed and touched by their obvious care and concern but remained ignorant of their shock at his skeletal appearance.

We joined my mother for her birthday on 16th May, even though Michael was not feeling well and wasn't his usual outgoing self. We were due to spend the remainder of our holiday with our son and his wife. What I did not notice was our daughter-in-law's reaction when she arrived to pick us up. As soon as she saw Michael, she was so shocked by his appearance that she quietly phoned Simon to warn him how ill he looked and to ask him to warn our granddaughters too.

The party was due to take place on 18th May at a venue quite close to my mother's house. Michael was too ill to attend but insisted that I went, so we arranged for him to rest at my mother's home and phone me if he had any problems. I could then enjoy the party but return quickly if needed.

Sadly, Michael's health deteriorated further and he was admitted to hospital. Without our knowledge, someone contacted Lucy and Jane in Australia to tell them that they needed to return to the UK urgently. We were not aware of this so when Michael heard that both our daughters were flying over from Australia, he downplayed his sickness and tried to persuade them not to come. His very gradual decline in health was probably the reason why I remained unaware of how ill he really was.

We spoke to the girls on Facetime supposedly a few hours before they flew out, but only a short while later I noticed Jane's husband and the children in the hospital and thought that I was seeing things. Michael protested that they should not have travelled so far just because he was not well and, as usual, stated that everyone was making a fuss over nothing. Several of the church elders also visited him. They, and other visitors, discovered that he had not lost his wonderful sense of humour and they frequently joked together. They nearly always left chuckling.

I walked alone to the Sunday morning service at CCK (Emmanuel Church). I arrived at the Clock Tower in the centre of Brighton and was trying to decide which way to go when God spoke very clearly to me. He said that we had been faithful in what we had been called to do and that now it was time to come back. I assumed that this word was for both of us and I was correct – in a way.

Ironically, at this church service, a friend of ours called Liz Woodgate told the congregation the story of how she had been healed of terminal oesophageal cancer (now detailed in her book, *Swallowed by Life*). Three years earlier Liz had emailed us in Australia explaining that she had been sent home to put her affairs in order as there was not anything else that could be done for her, and asking us to pray. Now she was cancer-free and able testify to God's healing power. Michael was where she had once been. I rejoiced with her but naturally had mixed emotions.

The next day Michael was admitted to the Martlets Hospice in Hove. The transfer process was exhausting, but two hours after arriving he still found the strength to talk to a visitor and his wife (both unbelievers) who arrived somewhat unexpectedly. This man was a former police colleague who our daughter Lucy had tracked down using her detective skills as Michael had said he would love to see him. About two years earlier he had also emailed us in Australia to ask us to pray for his wife, who had been diagnosed with terminal cancer but who was still alive and sitting beside him in a wheelchair. Seeing them there, Michael came to life and started sharing his Christian faith with them. It was wonderful to see him encouraging others to believe in Jesus which is something Lucy remembers so well. She was so proud of him that even though he was struggling to talk and his speech was slurred he was still preaching the gospel right up to the very end.

After this, Michael started to lose consciousness and seemed to be struggling. I felt that he was trying to hold on for me because he knew how hard it would be for me to live without him. We had been married for forty-eight years and had become a strong unit. I was not ready to let go and kept reassuring myself that God was going to heal him. But finally, when I saw him slipping in and out of consciousness, I spoke to him and encouraged him to let go. I just could not bear to see him suffer any more.

Michael had just passed away and I was sitting out in the gardens at the Martletts Hospice with the girls. I was trying to process that Michael had gone. Lucy had a book with her. It seemed like God's timing since at that moment there was a quote that jumped out at Lucy. It really helped me to understand and deal with the enormity of what had just happened. "What the caterpillar calls the end of the world, the master calls a butterfly". The caterpillar thinks it is dying and at the end of its life, but it is just the beginning as it starts a new life and turns into a beautiful butterfly. This is how I saw Mike's death, his earthly pain and body had now gone but his new eternal life was just beginning and that was something beautiful and lovely for Michael. I will see him again one day.

He died on 6th June 2013. The word to me at the Clock Tower about coming back was correct but it had its fulfilment in two different directions. Michael had 'come back' to the UK for good and I would have to go back to Australia on my own before returning to the UK permanently.

The last photo of Mike and I with our children. March 2011

Readjustment

The Thanksgiving Service for Michael was held at CCK (Emmanuel Church) on 17th June, the day after Fathers' Day in the UK which was especially hard for the children. Michael would have been amazed at the number of family members and friends who turned up to celebrate his life. The church building was packed and many of the people present had travelled a long way. One couple even interrupted their holiday in Devon and made a round trip of over four hundred miles just to be there. Michael was a very humorous person and several of the participants shared memories of the funny things that he had said or done. He would have loved the laughter and, more importantly, the sharing of his faith in Christ. It was a very joyful celebration.

I thought I was coping quite well until I faced the return flight to Perth on 28th June, just three weeks after Michael's death. Then it suddenly dawned on me that I had never flown anywhere without him. We had arrived in the UK together and now I was returning on my own. The impact of this was quite devastating and I struggled to cope. Simon accompanied me to the airport and spoke to one of the stewardesses, who upgraded me to first class and allowed me to take additional baggage because I was returning with some of Michael's possessions. She also stayed with me until I had taken my seat on the plane. I was so grateful to her.

The second part of my journey did not start off too well. I was under the impression that I could use the first-class lounge as I had been given a pass for it, but the stewardess on duty there would not let me go in because I did not have an appropriate ticket. As I was trying to explain the situation, and much to my surprise, my body went into total shock. On seeing this, another stewardess took me straight into the first-class lounge and stayed with me for the two-hour wait between flights. I was offered any food or drink that I wanted, but I opted only for tea and talked incessantly about Michael, which is probably what I needed to do. The stewardess ensured that I was fast-tracked to my seat and even gave me her email address so that I could tell her how I got on.

When I arrived in Perth I was met by some wonderful friends who drove me home. One of them went food shopping for me and another got the car started because the battery was flat. Naturally, it was hard to return to the house that Michael and I had planned together but I knew that I needed to face reality, however vulnerable I felt.

My friends did not think that I would cope on my own and, for the first two weeks, they were right. I could not stop crying and did not want to eat or do anything. Life just didn't seem worth living. People emailed me to say that they were praying for me and I could not understand why I felt so awful, so I asked God about it. The answer came straight back. He reminded me again of the time when, at age fourteen, I was not allowed to mourn the death of my little sister. My grief needed expression through tears. Suddenly, I realised that crying was not a shameful sign of weakness, but a positive activity that brought healing and release.

My parents lived through the Second World War in London where bombs were exploding night after night and people were dying all around them. Now I understood that the only way they could get through each day was to avoid facing up to their emotions. The problem was that I had been programmed to behave in the same way in peacetime. I simply copied them, crushed my feelings down inside and willed myself to get on with life. This had resulted in nearly thirty years of depression. I was now learning how important it was to grieve and let the emotion out through tears rather than crush it down and experience the resultant emotional problems.

I loved the way of life in Australia and really wanted to stay there. I battled with ways to achieve my goal but questioned whether this was really God's plan for me. The answer came from my Bible reading notes and a book I was reading called *Hosting the Presence* by Bill

Johnson. Bill talked about Kathryn Kuhlman, someone who had made a big impression on me when I had read her story a few years earlier. She recognised her need for absolute dependence on God and was totally surrendered to the Holy Spirit. I sensed that God was challenging me about obedience and those words 'trust' and 'obey' came to the fore again. I realised I was trying to persuade God to agree with me about Australia when he actually wanted me to return to the UK.

It is amazing how expert we are at reasoning over what God really did say! The day before Michael was transferred to the hospice, there was no doubt about his words to me. But now, a few weeks later, I was beginning to question his clear directive because I wanted to stay where I was. As soon as I gave up bargaining with him he gave me a fresh awareness of his peace and I, in turn, began preparing for the next adventure.

God honoured my willingness to let go in unexpected ways, notably financial. Michael's death had cost me quite a lot of money and for about three weeks I received nothing from his police pension. I was then informed that I would receive his full pension for three months. In addition, someone bought the scooter that he had been trying to sell for ages and I received $200 for recommending solar panels to a friend.

There was an enormous amount of stuff to sort out, particularly paperwork. It seemed that police personnel were encouraged to hold on to information and Michael's wallet was permanently crammed with scraps of paper bearing all sorts of scribbles that only he could decipher. I had to work out what was important and what was not. And when it came to clearing out the garage I discovered that he was an even bigger hoarder than I had imagined. He was however a tidy hoarder, almost squirrel-like. Lengths of rope were all tied neatly and hung up, while small items were stored away in drawers and little boxes. Michael's tidiness and organisational skills had evidently fooled me into thinking that he had less stuff in the garage than he actually had!

On 20th July we held a Thanksgiving Service for Michael in Perth. It was much harder the second time around. Not only was I having to go through the same event yet again, I was also aware that I could not move forward until our friends in Australia had been given the opportunity to say goodbye.

In all, 150 people turned up, which was quite amazing given the relatively short time that we had lived in Australia. Michael would have been amused by the physical appearance of his colleagues from the State Emergency Service. They usually attended formal functions wearing brown shirts and trousers, but they had been given special permission to dress in their work uniforms, namely bright orange jumpsuits. They said that Michael would have preferred that and they were right. He would also have been surprised that there was an official from FESA (Fire and Emergency Service Association) present. Excerpts recorded from the Brighton service were played and several friends from Perth shared their reflections about Michael. It was a wonderful happy service which doubtless he would have enjoyed too.

My birthday, at the end of July, was always going to be hard to enjoy. To take my mind off missing Michael my daughters whisked me off to buy a new watch, which would be from them and him. I usually keep watches for years, but my last one had somehow got lost because of recent hectic events. We had lunch out and dinner at one of their houses. It was a good day, much better than I had expected.

Sundays were the hardest days of all. At church services I was used to hiding behind Michael's extrovert personality, but now that he was not around I was somewhat exposed. As a result, I started feeling very low and it would often take me all week to regain my self-confidence. When faced with the possibility of attending a church day away I was not particularly enthusiastic, but decided that I needed to make the effort. While I was there people prayed for me and for more grief to be released. I returned feeling much stronger.

I was, however, in a lot of physical pain; a direct result of the stress and grief. I had physiotherapy and massages but my neck, shoulders and back were still in knots. One Sunday I went forward for healing. I had always found it hard to do that until I realised that I was being proud by thinking I did not need prayer. Happily, on this occasion, God met me. As people prayed for me I felt a tremendous heat flow slowly like a waterfall down my back to the bottom of my spine. As it travelled down, the pain left. It was an incredible experience. The next day I got out of bed with no ill effects for the first time in a long while. It struck me how easily I could have missed out on God's goodness if I had not been willing to take that first step forward.

As I started to sort things out in the garage I found a number of gadgets that Michael had stored in there. I had no idea what they were, or what they were used for so this presented me with a challenge. Up to now I had heard of people buying and selling items on the internet site Gumtree but had never used it myself. Someone helped me to get started and before long I was posting my belongings online. There is nothing like a new challenge! Not only did I sell several pieces of furniture, I also refused to be coerced into reducing the price. A couple of items completely foxed me. One was an air pressure thing and I was mystified as to its purpose so I took a photo of it and went to a local shop to see what it was worth. Then I copied onto Gumtree the wording from its box, added the photo and sold it. I did the same for the other item. Marvellous! God was teaching me how to live on my own.

The sale of Michael's bicycle was straightforward; the caravan posed the greatest challenge. I had never hooked it up to the car or towed it so I was understandably nervous on the day when I needed to transport it to the caravan yard.

A church elder was willing to tow the caravan but he was working when the yard was open, so I ended up having to master a new skill. The elder warned me about the extra width and length when driving around corners, and with his advice ringing in my ears, I set off – at about two miles per hour. I was not sure if the caravan would follow me but my rear-view mirror informed me that I had successfully managed to attach both vehicles together, which meant that I had overcome the first hurdle. My twelve-year-old grandson accompanied me and his comments 'You're doing great, Grandma' were a tremendous encouragement. He kept up this reassurance for the entire trip. I have to say I needed it. I knew that when we got to the Freeway (motorway) I would not be able to move into the fast lane to allow traffic to join us from the slip roads. But God helped me to regulate my speed and I was able to stay in the inside lane for the whole time.

The event that I was dreading soon arrived: turning off the freeway at a junction known to be very busy, with cars coming from all directions. However, when I arrived, much to my surprise and relief, the road was almost empty. The street where the caravan yard was situated was usually full of traffic but when I approached there was hardly a car in sight. I turned right into the yard and just abandoned both vehicles because I was so relieved at my safe arrival and totally exhausted too. Later I drove the car home, rejoicing at the way in which God had 'policed' everything for me.

Michael's birthday and those of our two grandsons were within a few days of each other in August, so we would often celebrate them together. My way of dealing with these difficult memories was to become occupied with other things, so on this occasion, I went to the Apple computer shop for an elementary lesson on my computer. 'How long have you had your laptop?' the class was asked. I was ashamed to say that I had had mine for nearly four years and still had not got beyond the basics. I soon realised that I did not only have to discover how to use my laptop, but also how to manage all the things that Michael would normally have dealt with.

My head was now starting to spin with all the information that I was trying to cram into it. There did not seem to be any more room and, like a computer, I was about to crash. From time to time computers need to be defragmented and I began to reason that the older you get, the more information you have gathered along the way and the more you need a periodic brain defragmentation.

The grief came in waves and I was struggling to cope. I emailed my sister and asked her how long it would go on. She had lost her husband to cancer and told me that two years was probably the minimum, which was not what I wanted to hear.

I went to hear a visiting preacher, who spoke about joy. His message had a big impact on me. I remember thinking, 'I need some of that.' He went on to say that if you have the Holy Spirit inside you, one of the fruits is joy. Then he invited people to go forward for prayer if they wanted more of the Holy Spirit. I went forward and as people prayed for me I felt such power fall on me that my legs almost gave way.

The following day I felt a bit tired and low but the intensity of grief that I had been carrying had gone. As I read my Bible I sensed God telling me that now was the time to move forward. He reminded me that I had a choice: to continue grieving and be sad or trust him and be joyful.

The next day I went to a barbecue breakfast, the first social event that I had attended on my own. It was a big step for me because I could not hide behind Michael, the extrovert with his natural sense of humour. Even though he was not with me I could still hear in my head the things he would say. I had a great time and soon afterwards I returned to my love of scrapbooking, which I had neglected when Michael had become ill.

The church's annual men's canoeing trip was held in October, after the hot weather had reduced the water levels to a safe depth. It was designed for the men to engage in bonding, and the year before Michael became sick, he had decided to turn the trip into a race. When he was the first to arrive, he humbly made sure that everyone knew about it!

This year there was a shortage of men who could go, so the trip was opened up to the women. I decided to take Michael's place and soon discovered that I was the only female, and the oldest person to have signed up. That was probably because the trip involved not only straight canoeing, but rapids as well, and these could be a bit scary. Eventually a couple of reluctant young women joined me, as did two from the YWAM base.

I would be competing in memory of Michael and I was determined to win and not let my gender or age defeat me. Having watched all the men fall out of their canoes at the bottom of the rapids, I elected to go down at a different angle. They all watched me from the bottom of each rapid section and I succeeded in staying in my canoe for the duration of the race. I took first place, although looking back, my success may well have been engineered.

October 31st would have been our forty-eighth wedding anniversary. Michael had become a Christian six months before our twenty-fifth anniversary and I recalled the amazing change in him then. Now I remembered our journey to the other side of the world and the joy and laughter that we had shared together. There was so much to be thankful for.

I continued to sort things out at home. The garage was Michael's domain and I had no idea what I should keep and what I should throw out. Were the tools really that essential? And would I use them or know what to do with them? Simon, who visited with his family, came to the rescue, declaring that most of the items were so old they were fit only for the bin.

In November I started planning visits to friends in Sydney and New Zealand before I returned to the UK. I was quite sad that Michael and I had not accepted an earlier invitation to New Zealand, but we did not know then what lay ahead. All the more reason to take the opportunity now. Michael was usually responsible for organising our trips so holidaying on my own was another big learning curve for me. This was something that I had never done before, and the memory of my trip back from the UK was still fresh in my mind.

When Simon and his family booked their Christmas holiday in Australia, no one imagined that Michael would not be around to enjoy it. They arrived on 10th December and it was lovely to entertain them at home, then go for a break in the south-west. We had a great time, but I found it hard entertaining the family without Michael. He was such an excellent host. And he was a terrific tour guide too, as we discovered when, without his natural sense of direction, we kept getting lost.

Simon and his family returned to the UK on 30th December. I had anticipated the challenge of returning to an empty house, so immediately after they had departed, I flew to Sydney for an eight-day break at the home of a friend of Simon's. This was followed by a two-week holiday visiting friends in New Zealand. In January I returned to Perth and put the house on the market.

Letting Go

I returned from New Zealand, thinking of the battles that lay ahead, and read this verse from 2 Chronicles 20:15: *'Do not be afraid! Don't be discouraged by this mighty army, for the battle is not yours, but God's'* (NLT). I knew that the sensible advice would be: 'Don't do anything rash so short a time after the death of a partner.' I ignored it. Eighteen months after we had moved into our new home, it was on the market.

I was acting on two things: Firstly, God had clearly told me to return to the UK, and secondly, the conviction that I should apply the lyrics of the song that had spoken to me back in 1984: 'Trust and obey, for there's no other way to be happy in Jesus, but to trust and obey'. It was a matter of trusting and obeying him regardless of what I or anyone else wanted, and not everyone thought that I was doing the right thing. I reasoned that God knew the road ahead and had plainly spoken to me, so in spite of people questioning 'Did God really say that?' I went ahead with my plans. The house sold quickly, although I remained in it until the transaction was completed.

I returned to the church that Michael and I had joined on our arrival in Australia. I struggled to resettle there and was often in tears during the worship. I would leave as soon as the service finished. It was hard to see God at work but that did not change the fact that there was a lot to organise and big decisions to make. Dealing with the finances alone was an enormous responsibility and although the recession in Europe had not affected Australia, I still needed financial advice when it came to transferring a large sum of money back to the UK. I just had to trust God, as we had done when we went to Australia in the first place.

The house and caravan had been sold, now it was time for the car. That was a significant challenge for me as it was a large four-wheel-drive

X-Trail which seemed even larger when it needed cleaning. Michael always did that and now I realised why he was always so pleased with the end result. First, I took it to the car wash, then I spent three hours finishing it off both inside and out so that it would be in pristine condition when I came to sell it. Michael, who had police experience of car dealers, always said they were never to be trusted and had shared many horror stories of criminal activity in relation to car sales. He was right. The price that I was offered was ridiculously low. Frankly, I was still grieving for Michael and just wanted to get rid of the vehicle, but I still decided to advertise it privately even though I knew that my decision was fraught with danger. But God was good to me.

A young English couple who had just arrived in Australia came to see the vehicle. I made sure that I had a male friend present to thwart any possible trickery, but in the event, they were more trusting than me. They were delighted with the car, made me a good offer, paid me a large cash deposit and transferred the balance into my bank account. This cleared before they collected the car.

I soon discovered that I had more belongings than I could ship in one container, so I had to be rigorous over what I needed and what I didn't. Suddenly my life was revolving around people who were in and out of my home, purchasing and collecting my possessions. The demands of relocating started to drain and overwhelm me. I lost sight of the way in which God uses the challenges of life to hone rather than to crush. But I came across some wise sayings that underlined this truth:

'Whether life grinds a man down or polishes him depends on what he's made of.'

'A diamond cannot be polished without friction, nor man made perfect without trials.'

'Great pilots are made in rough waters and deep seas.'

I had not been made strong by the good things that had happened to me but by the storms, winds and gales that had polished me. How dare I deny God the opportunity of refining my faith through difficulties? Once I decided to pray and leave my struggles with God,

I felt much better. I was also aware that I had some wonderful supportive friends in both countries. This knowledge was a great blessing which helped me through the pain and struggles.

Mastering grief was a gradual process. Sometimes I was up and sometimes down. The difficulty was to acknowledge the grief but not fall into self-pity – and also to understand the difference between the two. Psalm 1:2 exhorted me to delight in God's law and to meditate on it day and night. With this in mind, I tried to help myself by meditating on the Scriptures and applying them to my life.

Philippians 2:3–8 told me that I was called to have a humble and servant-like attitude, not looking only to my own interests but also to the interests of others. In my grief I was in danger of becoming very self-pitying because I was having to manage everything on my own without Michael. As a believer I knew that we were called to be like Christ, not only in our behaviour but also in our thoughts.

The most difficult area for me was my thought life. Psalm 5:11-12 (NLT) encouraged me in this: *'But let all who take refuge in you rejoice; let them sing joyful praises forever. Spread your protection over them, that all who love your name may be filled with joy. For you bless the godly, O Lord; you surround them with your shield of love'*. The choice was mine – to dwell on these words or to focus on my grief.

Michael may not have been there to advise me on selling things and organise my return to the UK, but God was an ever-present help if I allowed him to guide my thinking. He influenced my decisions in remarkable ways. For example, I knew that once I had sold the house, I would have to change a large quantity of Australian currency into Sterling. You could arrange an exchange rate in advance so I phoned to ask about this. Strangely, I did not feel peaceful about going ahead then, but a few days later, against the current trend, the rate had changed much more in my favour. God is so practical – a wonderful counsellor, you might say.

God continued to encourage me through the Bible on the run-up to my return to the UK. *'Don't worry about anything; instead, pray about everything. Tell God what you need, and thank him for all he has done. Then you will experience God's peace, which exceeds anything we can understand.*

His peace will guard your hearts and minds as you live in Christ Jesus' (Philippians 4:6–7 NLT). *'I will thank the Lord because he is just; I will sing praise to the name of the Lord Most High'* (Psalm 7:17 NLT).

I was delighted to see one of my grandsons baptised on 9th March, three weeks before my trip. The sale of the house was completed on March 14th and on 1st April I was back in the UK. How quickly things moved!

A wonderful friend called Jacquie invited me to stay with her while I looked for a new home. I was not too sure where to go, so I visited all the estate agents between Brighton and Shoreham because that was where I had lived for most of my life. It was a very large region, which did not help me to make a decision. When Jacquie said that she thought I needed to reduce my search area, I immediately said, 'Southwick', a town that was not even on my mind. We went straight there and visited all the estate agents, the last of which came up trumps. The agent had just returned from measuring up two properties and I made appointments then and there to view them. The first one had been modernised; the second one was an executor's sale and needed bringing up to date. As soon as I saw the latter I knew that it was the right place for me.

Six weeks after returning to the UK I had my new home. I picked up the keys on 20th May, but needed to have some work done before I moved in. Meanwhile, my shipping container arrived and was placed in storage until I was housed. I cannot explain it, but when you trust God he has a plan that you won't always understand.

Since arriving back I was visiting different churches to see where God wanted me to worship. The church that Michael and I had been attending before we went to Australia had changed and I did not feel it was right to return there. After I had tried a dozen churches, my friends Dave and Rosie invited me to join them at King's Church in Horsham and even arranged a lift there for me as I had no transport. I had a great sense of peace there and just knew that it was the right church for me. I arranged to return the following week but realised that if I was going to attend regularly I would need a car.

I just required a small car to get around in, so the next morning I phoned a friend to see what he would recommend. He investigated this and phoned back to say that he had found a car and had arranged for someone to bring it round to my house for a test drive at midday. The two-year-old ex-mobility automatic car was in excellent condition, had done only 3,000 miles and drove extremely well. My friend negotiated the purchase over the phone and in a matter of hours it was mine. I could not believe what had just happened. Before Michael bought a vehicle he would go from garage to garage, look at all the chassis numbers and check that the vehicles were not registered stolen before committing himself to a purchase. I looked skywards and said, as if to him, 'You won't believe what I've just done.' Clearly God was intent on looking after me.

Naturally, I kept asking myself why God had found me a home in Southwick when I would be involved in a church twenty-four miles away. It did not seem to make sense as I felt that God was in both decisions. Slowly things started to become clearer. If I had moved directly to Horsham, I would have kept returning to my friends further south, which would have made it much harder to settle. God arranged for many of those I already knew in the Southwick area to support me through the continuing grief and readjustment. I went to their midweek home groups, some of which were focused on worship and Bible study while others were socially orientated. Only after I had made new friends in the Horsham church would I move to the Horsham area.

After eleven months in the UK, I returned to Australia to visit friends and family and to enjoy some sunshine in the middle of the British winter! Obviously it was hard to go without Michael because we had always travelled together. I had to change planes in Dubai and as we were in transit an elderly lady struck up a conversation with me. While we waited in the airport she told me that she was eighty-five years old and that she visited her daughter in Perth every year. Apparently, her friends and family had questioned whether she should still be travelling so far on her own at her age. She then said to me, 'It's all an attitude of mind, dear.' She did not realise the impact these words would have on me. Without knowing it, she was helping me out of the self-pity that I was feeling at having to travel on my own. It was as though God had put her in the seat in front to share her positive attitude with me. The second part of the journey was going to take ten hours but she simply said, 'By the time you've watched a few films, you're there.' I certainly learnt something about attitudes from this little old lady who trotted happily around Dubai Airport confidently paying for refreshments on her credit card. I, by contrast, had no idea how to pay for things in a different currency.

Without Michael there did not seem much point in celebrating my seventieth birthday in July. Then God spoke to me about having a party to thank all my friends and family who had been there for me since I had returned to the UK. I was suddenly aware of how blessed I was to be surrounded by such wonderful people who freely let me pop into their homes for a cup of tea and a chat – a lifeline at times. Lucy came over from Australia to celebrate with me and we had a brilliant time. Michael would normally have stood up and thanked everyone for being there, but I surprised myself by taking over from him. I publicly expressed great gratitude to everyone for helping me through this difficult time. I was stepping forward into a new confidence.

An overwhelming sense of grief came over me again, even two years after Michael's death. One Sunday morning I went forward after the meeting and asked for prayer to be refilled with the Holy Spirit. Two women came and prayed with me but they discerned that what I really needed was prayer in relation to grief. I had not shared with either of them what I was going through, but both were 'spot on' in what they said. One of them told me that the grief was coming to an end and encouraged me to put my hand on my heart and let it go. As she spoke I felt a physical pain inside, which I had not felt before. They advised me to go home, cry to God and tell him how I felt about all that had happened. But since I was en route for a conference in Bedford I could not follow through on their counsel.

It was the first time that I had attended a conference without Michael and I also had to stay in a Travelodge on my own. On the first day, while we were worshipping, I sensed that God wanted me to take off

Michael's wedding ring. Two days before he died it had fallen off his finger because he had lost so much weight, so for safekeeping, I had put it on my finger along with my ring. It had stayed there for more than two years. I did not find it easy to take off because I was dealing with so much emotion but I really wanted to be obedient to what God was saying. First, I put it in my trouser pocket, then I had the sense that God did not want me to keep it on my person, so I put it in my handbag.

During the next time of worship God challenged me about Michael's ashes, which were sitting in a cupboard in the lounge. I had told myself that other things were a far higher priority, but maybe I was actually holding on to what I had left of him. It was emotionally hard to let him go, but as the worship continued I was able to say yes to God that I would attend to Michael's ashes.

After my return from the conference the grief hit me again and seemed worse than ever. It was then I remembered what had been said to me about my crying out to God over the pain inside. There was a lot to remember: Michael's diagnosis only a week after we had moved to our new home; the months of treatment; having to feed him through a tube; major surgery; the shock of seeing him in intensive care with tubes and wires attached to him; thinking he was getting better; the distress at discovering that he still had cancer; the chemotherapy and radiation treatment and the long-distance travelling from our house to the hospital. I poured all this out to God and felt a huge sense of relief. It was as though a weight was being lifted off me.

Two days later I realised that my Facebook photo showed Michael and me together, so I replaced it with a happy one of me on my own. As I went to close down my computer I suddenly realised that Michael was also on my screensaver, so I updated that too.

It would have been so easy to cling to past memories and grief, but God was changing me from the inside and I was trying hard to be a willing participant in his plan for my future. Certainly, the memories were still there, but the debilitating pain was giving way to an incredible inner joy. I had married Michael when I was just twenty years old and we had promised to stay together until 'death do us part'. Now death had parted us, and letting go seemed the natural thing to do. I was starting to move on.

Since Michael had been in the Royal Navy and the sea was in his blood, I had it in mind to scatter his ashes at sea. I made arrangements with the Royal Navy and a few weeks later I took the urn to the railway station en route for Portsmouth, where Michael and I had lived for the first ten years of our marriage. As I walked down the road I was suddenly struck by the humour of my situation. Here was I carrying a shopping bag with Michael's ashes in it, as if I were accompanying him on his last walk; and he was heavy! I knew that he would have found it very funny as well. It was as though he was there with me and we were enjoying the trip together.

I shared this humorous thought with the friend who met me at Portsmouth Station. We had known each other for about forty-five years and we laughed together as we delivered Michael's ashes to HMS *Nelson* before we went out for lunch. Due to some bad storms the scattering of the ashes had to be postponed for a month. Simon came with me for the Ceremony. The Navy did a lovely service on board before scattering his ashes, but what amazed me was exactly where they were dispersed. Michael had always been fascinated by naval history and showed a keen interest in the raising of the *Mary Rose*. He would have been delighted to know that his ashes were scattered at the exact place where this ship had originally been lying. I discovered that, as his wife, I was entitled to have my own ashes distributed at sea, and I arranged for this to be done in the same place. I reasoned that it would be a comfort to our children to know that our ashes were together.

A New Vision

Michael was planning to mark 31ˢᵗ October 2015, our fiftieth wedding anniversary, with a celebratory cruise. I decided against the temptation to be consumed by self-pity and spent the morning at the church's quarterly 'Ladies that Breakfast' event. This was followed by afternoon tea in a hotel with a friend; a birthday gift from one of my brothers. We had a great time remembering some of the fun times that we and our husbands had shared together.

When Jane discovered that I had no plans to celebrate Christmas she invited me to return to Australia to spend time with her family and Lucy. I had only been back in the UK for about eight months but the idea of sun, sea and sand somehow appealed to me, so within twenty-four hours I had bought my return ticket for a six-week trip. I had three weeks to buy Christmas cards and presents, pay the bills and generally get myself ready to go.

Since Michael's death I had begun to think differently about the future. I reflected more on the uncertainty of life in relation to my health and what I could afford. There would probably come a day when I wouldn't be able to travel so far and I did not want to waste time dithering about when I could afford to go away.

I stayed in three different locations: one with each of my daughters and another with some friends. First, I was with Jane and her family. We spent a week on Rottnest Island off the west coast of Australia opposite Fremantle. It's a car-free zone, so walking or cycling was the order of the day. Tandem-riding with my grandson was great fun and quite relaxing. He sat in front and did most of the hard work, although I helped out here and there. When we went downhill I found my legs would not go round fast enough so I simply stuck them out each side.

Then I spent a few days with Lucy at Busselton, known for its famous timber jetty, which is nearly two miles long. I was even able to borrow a car for a week, which was an added bonus. I couldn't deny that I felt as though I had come home. I loved the climate and lifestyle and seriously began wondering if I should return to Australia. Friends took me to look at new homes and plots of land by the Indian Ocean, trying to get me to move back. Admittedly, the views were magnificent – clear blue skies and miles of soft white sand – picture perfect, just like you see in the holiday brochures. Who would not want to stay?

Vision for the New Year – that seemed to be the topic of conversation among my Australian friends and in the churches too. The New Year seemed to usher in new hope and a new beginning. At first, I did not share this enthusiasm. For me 2016 was just another pointless twelve months to get through without Michael.

Then God reminded me of something that he had said to me back in 1996, twenty years before, when I had been healed of cancer. At that time, he had encouraged me to write a book about my story of faith through pain. While I was living in Australia I had made what I considered a big effort, but that amounted to only one A4 page. My early attempt seemed pathetic, so I decided to make a concerted effort to work on the book through the coming year. This new vision gave me a fresh sense of excitement about the future, a real joy bubbling up from inside.

I arrived back in the UK in January, knowing that this was where I was meant to be. Maybe I had needed to return to Australia and the life that Michael and I had so loved before I could get to the point of contentment at home and making the most of life on my own.

At first, I assumed that I would relocate to Horsham in July 2017. This was because I was collecting my granddaughter from school while her parents were working. At the end of term, she would be moving to secondary school, so July seemed the obvious time to move until my daughter-in-law commented, 'If you're going to move anyway, why wait?' Her throwaway comment triggered something in me, and I felt it was ok to move sooner.

I pondered what she had said for about a week and then attended the Prophetic Academy at King's Church the following Saturday. I chatted to someone there about my thoughts on moving and he challenged me to put my name down with an estate agent in Southwater, just south of Horsham. Southwater properties were cheaper than in Horsham and a number of other church members also lived there. During the lunch break I registered with an estate agent and chatted to people the following day at church about the decision to put my property on the market.

That evening, I hoed the front garden, cleared the weeds on the patio in the back garden and spruced up the lounge. At 9:00am the next day I phoned several estate agents to arrange valuations and spent the rest of the day cleaning. By Thursday the photos were ready, by Friday they were on the internet and on Saturday the first viewer was looking around. Everything was moving so quickly; except the writing of this book!

Two weeks later I was due to catch up with a friend in Eastbourne but she was not feeling well, so we postponed our meeting. Instead, I went to an event in Southwick village where I bumped into another friend who had been away. She was surprised to learn that I was selling the bungalow earlier than expected and told me that she knew of someone who might be interested.

Then and there she phoned her friend, who came down from London the following day to visit her sister and view my property. As soon as she had seen my house she made an offer, which she increased to the full asking price because she was so keen on it. It struck me that these 'chance events' would never have taken place had the day in Eastbourne not been cancelled. Somehow, I was unconsciously in tune with the promptings of God.

At another church prophetic training day in early July, I was given a very encouraging prophetic word: 'You're the Lord's rose – amazing at making things. God declares that you are in his hands and have been through a season of pruning and preparation, of pulling off the thorns, removing the things that you'd expect to be there for protection or security and making you open and vulnerable. This is the way he wants it to be. He's putting a group around you who are not only for you, but also for your heart and vision. He wants to celebrate your faithfulness and perseverance. And, just like an exhibitor at the Chelsea Flower Show, he intends to show the world how amazing his rose is, so that many will know who you are and be drawn to him. He loves you; he's your proud Father.'

I was reminded of a word that I was given in 2004, long before I was considering moving to Australia: 'I can see a picture of a clear glass vase with a beautiful rose in it. You're the rose and God is restoring what the locust has taken. God will give back in abundance. Continue to be transparent, don't let others close you down. You're a beautiful rose.' Someone else at the same training day added, 'Age isn't important. The best is yet to come. There's so much more to come.'

When others, who have no idea of my struggles, share these things with me, it is a real confirmation that God knows and cares. Their words inspire me, particularly when my life seems to be battle-orientated and when I am tempted to feel worthless as an older member of society. Either I listen to the world's assessment or I look to God and keep trusting him.

My move to Southwater involved a few ups and downs but I was finally installed in February. I loved my new home and decided that I would live in it for a year before I made any major changes to it.

I completed the Prophetic Academy course in 2016 and offered to help with the refreshments in 2017. This meant that I was able to hear the teaching again and to take part in one of the workshops. Strangely, I was persuaded to go to the writing workshop, which would not be a normal choice for someone with dyslexia. We ended the session by asking two questions of God: 'What are you excited about today?' and 'What are your dreams for me?' We then wrote down our replies. I was amazed not only at what I wrote, but also at how my writing just flowed. Over the next two weeks I found that I was expressing things more easily on paper, which was great news in light of the fact that I was trying to write this book.

In the event, I did not wait a year to make major changes to my home because after I had been in it a few months I was keen to put my stamp on it. Naturally, I spent loads of time planning and although someone else carried out the significant work, I did much of the decorating afterwards. My new home has an additional door to the lounge for easier exiting and more light, a kitchen/dining room instead of two rooms and a new kitchen. Living in the mess was not easy, but I survived and the work was completed by the end of the year. I surveyed the scene and then started musing on what else in the house needed decorating. I stopped adding to my list when God reminded me about the book again and I decided that I would do no more to the house until I had finished working on the book.

At the beginning of January 2018, the Sunday morning preacher began his sermon by repeating the words, 'battles and blessings' over and over. He wanted to make a memorable and profound point and it certainly had an impact on me. His message considered the way we expect a period of blessing to go on forever without the battles that will inevitably accompany it.

I looked at the last few years of my life and agreed with what he said. Michael and I had obeyed God and gone to the other side of the world. Yes, he had blessed us there, but the move came at a cost because we had to leave our family and friends behind. We had some great times in Australia but Michael's sickness took its toll too.

One of the hardest battles that I had to face was doing everything on my own without having Michael with me to share the load. I had to depend on God to help me and he never let me down. So here was another new year and God had blessed me with a wonderful house in Southwater and a church that I loved. But I had to remember that there would still be daily battles to go through too.

I am discovering that the biggest conflict is the battle for the mind. I have come through years of depression, major health issues and grief, but I have realised that we have a choice in the way we think. Michael always used to talk about positive thinking, which he practised throughout his life. I struggled to understand this because my mind was naturally predisposed to negativity. It was far easier for me to see the bad than the good in any given circumstance.

Helpful Christian books tell us that 'what you think is what you become'. This highlights the importance of thinking God's thoughts, not our own. The Bible is God's instruction manual on life and it says:

'As [a man] thinks in his heart, so is he.' (Proverbs 23:7 NKJV).

'We take captive every thought to make it obedient to Christ.' (2 Corinthians 10:5).

'Whatever is true, whatever is noble, whatever is right, whatever is pure, whatever is lovely, whatever is admirable – if anything is excellent or praiseworthy – think about such things.' (Philippians 4:8).

Everyone has a will – a place where we choose to meditate on or discard a thought. In principle, this is a simple idea; in practice, it is not so easy. If you are a negative-thinking person, you will want to hang onto negative thoughts and your emotions will become negative too. But if you think positively your emotions will follow suit.

Thoughts are powerful and affect our lives. One person can have all the advantages of a good upbringing and yet be a thoroughly pessimistic individual. Similarly, another person can have a horrible upbringing or serious health issues and yet have a very happy attitude to everything. Proverbs 17:22 tells us, *'A cheerful heart is good medicine, but a crushed spirit dries up the bones.'*

Romans 12:2 tells us to be transformed by the renewing of our minds. It is interesting to note that some doctors have discovered we are able to renew our minds because the brain has the ability to change itself for better or worse. Either we become lazy and allow anything into our heads, or we control our thought life, think right and act right as a result. This has been one of the most important lessons that I have learnt in my walk with God.

Taking Off the Grave Clothes

I had always found it hard to understand why the Israelites wandered around in the wilderness for forty years when they could have reached the Promised Land in eleven days. Since I had become a Christian I had always tried to obey God when I heard from him, so I was somewhat surprised when he seemed to suggest that I was roaming in the desert. How exactly was I roaming?

When Lazarus had been in the tomb for four days, Jesus raised him from the dead and commanded the onlookers, *'Take off the grave clothes and let him go'* (John 11:44). Yes, God had raised me from death to life, but was I still wearing the grave clothes? And if so, what were they in my case? I had been through a lot since Michael's death and thought that I was doing well – apart from the odd hiccup, of course.

As I meditated on the words *'Take off the grave clothes'*, it struck me that much of my present identity was still connected with Michael. Certainly I had been able to jump over many of the hurdles that had defeated me in my early life: feelings of insecurity and worthlessness, my perceived lack of intelligence, the belief that others didn't want to know me because I was not good enough, and the conviction that I had nothing to offer. Michael had a magnetic and funny personality which drew others to him, so when we were man and wife I reckoned that it was not me they wanted to know, but him. I was just an add-on.

Emotionally I needed to step out of my grave clothes (the continuing, if unconscious relationship with Michael) and into freedom in Christ. No longer must I allow my past experiences to shape my present and future. I needed to become the unique person that God wanted me to be.

As I read 1 Thessalonians 5:16-22 (NKJV) seven directives stood out:

1. Rejoice always.

2. Pray without ceasing.

3. In everything give thanks; for this is the will of God in Christ Jesus for
   you.

4. Do not quench (extinguish) the Spirit.

5. Do not despise prophecies.

6. Test all things; hold fast to what is good.

7. Abstain from every form of evil.

All seven aspects of these verses speak of choice. I get up in the morning and choose either to rejoice over what every new day holds for me, or rehearse how badly I have been treated in the past and get stuck where I am. Joy is the fruit of the Spirit and is proof of the presence of God in my life. As such, it must become a habit. *'This is the day the Lord has made; we will rejoice and be glad in it'* (Psalm 118:24 NKJV)

The apostle Paul says, *'Don't copy the behavior and customs of this world, but let God transform you into a new person by changing the way you think. Then you will learn to know God's will for you, which is good and pleasing and perfect'* (Romans 12:2 NLT).

My experiences in life have shaped the way I think and it's often simpler for my mind to revert to the old thought patterns. To change the metaphor, it's much easier to follow the same hardened tyre tracks that you have always used than to forge a new track altogether. It's when I face difficulties that I am prone to think negatively and believe that I can't do something. And in social situations I can easily withdraw and feel that I have nothing to offer.

Happily I have discovered that change isn ot so hard when my mind is fixed on Jesus and when I'm determined to believe Scripture rather than the old learnt patterns of behaviour.

Proverbs 3:5 says *'Trust in the Lord with all your heart, and lean not on your own understanding'* (NKJV). Trusting God is not a one-off event. It is something that we need to do all the time. I have tried to learn how to talk to him as I go through each day, asking him what he wants me to do. Sometimes he does not direct me as I would expect. Occasionally he indicates that he would like me to visit someone and it is often when I am tired and would simply prefer to stay at home. Similarly, I can be mid-conversation with someone and he will give me the words that cut straight to the root of a situation or problem.

Steadily I am leaving behind the grave clothes, listening to that still, small voice and trying to follow it. It is a step-by-step process which leads to an increased ability to hear God and a growing confidence in what he is saying.

God does things in his own unique way and blesses those who keep their eyes on him. Isaiah says, *'"For My thoughts are not your thoughts, nor are your ways My ways," says the Lord. "For as the heavens are higher than the earth, so are My ways higher than your ways, and My thoughts than your thoughts"'* (Isaiah 55:8–9 NKJV). *'You will keep in perfect peace all who trust in you, all whose thoughts are fixed on you!'* (Isaiah 26:3 NLT).

The world's way is often about fixing your thoughts on yourself and about believing what others say about you. That is the way to anxiety and sometimes even to suicide. God calls us to spend time with him, to understand our identity in Christ and to know what his Word says about us. God encouraged Joshua, *'Study this Book of Instruction continually. Meditate on it day and night so you will be sure to obey all that is written in it. Only then will you prosper and succeed'* (Joshua 1:8 NLT). Success comes with meditation and obedience and this involves practice and the desire and commitment to change.

After one Sunday morning church service, I was trying to work out whether I should make my way home for a quick lunch or go out for a roast meal. I opted for the roast and decided to go to the local garden centre for it. I ordered and sat with my back to the wall so that I could see everyone else who was there. I watched couples and larger family groups as they ate and chatted together, then I had my own lunch and for the first time I felt no sense of rejection or isolation. I was just content that God had brought me through to a new place of peace.

Left to my own devices, I would have gone straight home after the meal, but as I left I sensed that I should visit some friends whom I had not seen for a while. The husband had been through two years of sickness which had put a strain on his wife. She shared with me the past few months of their journey and told me that they were both exhausted. I related easily to the situation because I had gone through something similar with Michael. Two hours later, the wife told me how much better she was feeling and expressed her gratitude to me for stopping by. She also thanked me for helping her to see their next step. I went home happy that I had been able to discern God's voice and feeling good just knowing that my experiences had blessed someone else. God does not waste our difficulties, but uses them to help the next person on their journey.

Along with the renewal of my mind has come a renewal of my energy levels. In the past I would get overtired, which would make me feel low and unable to cope. Instead of stopping and resting I would continue until I had nothing left and was completely exhausted.

For example, I have a lot of lawn around my house and mowing it is a big job which used to take most of the day. I would start off enthusiastically and get slower and slower as my energy levels waned and I wilted. Now I do not feel the need to complete the whole job in one go. I am happy to do it as and when I feel that I have the time and strength. I give myself permission to rest, recognising that I don't need to be constantly working. Maybe it is something that I learnt from my brother who lives in Spain. He has his siesta after lunch as the Spanish do.

I am so grateful to God for making me content to be the person that I am. I used to worry about what others thought of me, but now I am secure in him and feel no pressure to perform. My identity is now in the Lord and not in being Michael's wife.

Many years ago, God spoke to me about writing a book. This was a near impossibility for someone who was dyslexic and had appalling spelling and non-existent computer skills, plus a terrible lack of self-confidence. But I pressed on and with patience and dogged determination, and most of all with His help, I have finally done as he asked. I am so grateful to Him for all the wonderful things he has done in my life. If he can do the impossible for me, he can do it for anyone, and I am excited to find out what lies ahead.

God has been so faithful and done so much more in my life than I could ever imagine. Joy really did come in the morning!

A new joy is coming. Australia December 2019

Reflections

Throughout this book, Mary has touched on different life challenges that sadly are common to a lot of people. The following pages have a number of questions that you might want to consider further, in quiet moments of reflection. At the end of the questions for each chapter, there is a prayer you could pray.

Chapter 1

Mary gave us insights into the influences that shaped her during her childhood. The following questions look at some of the things that may have influenced you growing up. For example: a lack or excess of money; poor communication, lack of affection, fun or even an abusive, controlling family life.

1. Think about the type of parents you had and their personalities. How has that influenced the person you are?

Positives:

Negatives:

2. Think about the attitude of others around you. For example, in your school life, sports and activities, friendships - were you encouraged, praised or criticised?

Positives:

Negatives:

3. Highlight and share some of the other influences that shaped your childhood and the person you have become.

Positives:

Negatives:

Prayer

Heavenly Father I thank you for all the good things that my parents did for me, provided for me, despite their own weaknesses and battles. I chose to forgive them for the times when things did not go well, the pain it caused to me, and the lasting effect that has had. Today, I bring these negative experiences to you and ask for the ability to let go of them, to receive your healing and freedom that was won on the cross and through your resurrection. As I allow you to release the pain and trauma from my life, I receive in exchange both healing and wholeness from you, in order to be the person you designed and created me to be. Amen.

Chapter 2

1. How do you communicate? Have you followed your parents' style of communication?

Positives:

Negatives:

2. Do you pray about the daily 'nitty-gritty'?

3. In what ways have you been afraid for others to see the 'real' you?

4. In what areas do you battle fear and insecurity in everyday life and in relationships?

5. How do you trust and obey God in your life? Where is trust a battle for you?

6. In what ways is God asking you to take a step forward?

Prayer

Thank you, Lord Jesus, that you conquered fear, insecurity, inferiority and intimidation so that I can live free from these areas in my life. Where I battle with these areas, I ask for you to expose the roots and lies that hold them in place, and for the courage to deal with them. I want to live a life of courage and strength and receive them as a gift in exchange for the battles. In the coming weeks, please let me see big or small answers to this prayer. Amen.

Chapter 3

Some Bible readings Mary wrote about:

2 Corinthians 5:17; Romans 8:28; Ephesians 6:16; Hebrews 12:5–11; Romans 12:2; John 15:4; John 15:2

1. Mary is very honest about her long-term struggle with depression. In what areas of your life have you or do you struggle? How has God been helping, teaching and challenging you?

2. As you look back at your life, when you have wondered where God is and how did you handle these times?

3. Like Mary selling the caravan, has God asked you to do something you did not want to do? How did you obey?

4. Mary started to realise the importance of her thought life. What controls your thought life?

5. Like Mary did, do you find your self-worth in what you do rather than who you are? Where do you gain your self-worth from? How is your sense of identity linked to what you do or what you have achieved?

Prayer

Father God, I thank you for making me your child and forgive me where I have performance and activity as my identity and value in life, rather than in simply being your child. Where there is imbalance between performance & rest, between your unconditional love for me and seeking the reward and acknowledgement of others in my life, I ask for your help to make the changes needed to bring balance to my life, as well as physical and emotional healing. Amen.

Chapter 4

1. Identify a new season you faced in life. How did you cope with its challenges and what did you learn?

2. What mask are you wearing (e.g. respectability, lack of confidence, making out you are OK when things are wrong)?

3. When Mary was dealing with fear, she turned to Isaiah 43:18–19, which tells us not to remember the former things, that God is doing a new thing. What areas of your life cause you fear?

4. 1 Peter 5:6-7 says to cast all our worries and cares on God because He cares for us. What things are you carrying that you need to give to God?

Prayer

Heavenly Father, thank you for not giving me a spirit of fear but giving love, peace and a sound mind. Where I battle with fear, worries and the cares of everyday life, I hand them over to you and ask for you to deal with each one. I ask for your help to let go of them and help not to pick them up again tomorrow! Please intervene on my behalf in the everyday challenges, big and small, so I have my own testimony of victories, just as Mary has. Amen.

Chapter 5

Some Bible readings: Psalm 27:4; Romans 8:37

1. When has God given you someone to work alongside you in an area where you are weak? Was that a help or a challenge for you?

2. Asking to be anointed with oil was challenging for Mary but she did it in obedience to God's word. How prepared would you be to step out in faith for something God's word commands you to do?

3. Mary shares the amazing joy and peace she felt before the start of her chemotherapy treatment. Can you share an occasion when you experienced joy and peace in spite of adverse circumstances?

4. Mary was humbled by the prayers of others for her. Are we prepared to ask for prayer and be humble enough to be open about your needs?

5. Do you rush in with answers to other people's needs, without realising that your desire to rescue reflects your own need?

6. Do you really KNOW God's love in every area of life? Or is there any area where you have struggled to receive forgiveness?

7. Are we prepared to trust God in areas such as finance, when it does not seem to make sense to do so?

Prayer

Thank you, Jesus for all the times I can look back and see the times you answered my prayers, helped me in difficult situations, and brought people into my life to help in different ways. I ask for your help today to trust you more in situations, relationships, struggles I am facing. Act on my behalf and also show me changes I need to make to see the answers I long for. Grant me peace to wait for answers and peace in the storms of life. Amen.

Chapter 6

Some Bible readings, based on passages Mary wrote about:
Philippians 4:13; Matthew 5:9; Romans 5:1–5; Jeremiah 33:6

1. What does 'I can do all things through Christ who strengthens me' mean to you? When have you needed to persevere?

2. James 1:2–5 tells us to *'count it all joy ... whenever you face trials of many kinds...'* Psalm 100 also challenged Mary's attitude to joy. Trials bring out our true character. Are we allowing God to test us?

3. Just as Mary and Michael experienced supernatural joy as they sought God during the challenges of cancer, do you experience the joy that God's Word promises when going through trials?

4. Computing was a skill Mary needed to learn. What skill (skills) does God want you to learn?

5. Are you willing to let go of an area or issue that has dominated your life, to make sure that your identity is in Christ alone?

6. Using Mary's illustration of an iceberg, think about your life or relationships. How much is hidden? How much is exposed? Satan has no power once things are brought into the light.

7. Mary still has to battle with fear. How do you feel about fear and pride (and the link between the two)?

8. In Judges 6:11–16 Gideon felt insignificant. We only find true significance when we trust and obey God. Can you trust God when what he is asking seems way beyond your ability?

Prayer

Father God, HELP! I face challenges between what I want, what you desire, and what others need from me. Help me change where I need to make adjustments; strengthen me so I can be strong in areas where I am currently weak or where I need to press on in a difficult situation; show me how to deal with new circumstances, relations and pressure. Let me experience your love, peace and joy in new ways. Amen.

Chapter 7

Some Bible readings, based on passages Mary wrote about:
John 10:10; Ephesians 5:22; Hebrews 11:8; Joshua 1:8–9; Genesis 19:26; Luke 17:32; 1 Chronicles 4:9–10; Isaiah 54:2–3

1. What has been the biggest challenge God has faced you with? How did you react?

2. Have you experienced God's financial provision? How did this affect your faith?

3. Meditating on Bible verses we believe God has given us can encourage and strengthen us. Which verses are special to you? What words and promises have helped you keep going through challenging times?

4. Mary mentions that getting together all the papers required for their visa application in such a short time was 'against all the odds'. Does this remind you of something that has happened to you? When?

5. How encouraged do you feel as you read of the rapid sale of Michael and Mary's house? What does it say to you about how God can lead and provide?

6. Mary spoke of God being her Healer, Friend, Shield, etc. What has God been to you?

7. The move of BOTH Mary's daughters to Australia is surprising. What experiences do you have of God's generosity?

Prayer

Heavenly Father, thank you that you are interested in the small and large things in my life. Thank you for acting on my behalf in ways I will never see or know, to protect, provide and bless me. With all that I am dealing with at the moment, I proclaim your sovereignty and authority over all that is happening. As Jesus taught us, I pray that "Your Kingdom come, Your will be done" in every area of my life and my world. Surprise me in the coming weeks in ways that I know is you acting on my behalf as you did for Mary and help me not to miss the little answers too! Amen.

Chapter 8

1. God prepared Mary for what was to come, giving her incredible joy in the face of tough challenges. How have you known the truth of Nehemiah 8:10: *'the joy of the Lord is your strength'*?

2. When you were faced with difficult circumstances, what did you find helpful?

3. The work done at Michael and Mary's new home by their local church was an unexpected blessing. If your church helps others in need, what might you be able to contribute?

4. It took six years for Mary to realise that God answered her question only six weeks later! Have you missed answers to prayer because the answers weren't what you were looking for?

Prayer

Thank you, Jesus that like the disciples, you are with us in storms, having promised to *never leave us or forsake us*. Thank you for every person and organisation that has helped, encouraged and supported me in big and small ways when I was in need. Whilst I wait for you to answer my prayers and needs, I ask that you show me one person each week that I can help, encourage or support & help me to be your hands and feet and hugs to them. Amen.

Chapter 9

Following Michael's death Mary had to deal with a lot of grief.

1. Working through grief was a gradual process for Mary. What practical and spiritual steps did you notice in her journey through this stage?

2. What characteristics of grief have you noticed in your own or others' experience?

3. Has there been a time when you felt prompted to let go of something from the past? Was it a battle? Did you let go or did you hold on to it?

4. How ready are you to be honest when there is a call to receive prayer? Are you missing God's blessing by thinking 'That's for others!' or 'I'm OK'?

5. Mary is eternally thankful for Michael even though he's not with her each day & for the blessing of their three children. Why not look back on your life to see what you can be thankful for?

Prayer for Grief and Loss

Father God, the hymn writer got it right when he wrote "How great the pain of searing loss…" and I know that you felt the same when Jesus died, for me. Would you come into my life today and heal the pain that at times overwhelms me. Thank you for all the happy times and blessing of the relationship but I need you to fill the void left inside me from my loss. I need you to help me day by day to move forward in life and know your love, joy and gentleness. Surround me with those who will encourage, support and at times provoke me to action, so that my life is complete in a different way. Amen.

Chapter 10

Some Bible readings, based on passages Mary wrote about:
2 Chronicles 20:15; Psalm 1:2; Philippians 2:3-8; Philippians 4:6-7; Psalm 7:17

1. How do you 'hear God'? Have you acted on what he says even when it seems ridiculous? Be honest.

2. Read Psalm 5:11-12. How do you feel about this in relation to your life? Mary's choice was to focus on her grief or to let go of it. How do you apply this to the situation you face or have faced in life?

3. It was so clear God had his hand on Mary's life – providing her with a place to live, a church to attend, the right car to buy and special encounters. When did you clearly experience God's hand on your life?

4. Mary came to the realisation that she needed to let go of Michael (by taking off his wedding ring and releasing his ashes). Are there things NOW that God wants you to relinquish?

Prayer

Heavenly Father, thank you for every time I can look back and see you at work in my life and in the lives of those around me. Thank you that I can hear your voice and I ask to sharpen my hearing and to have the courage to act on what I hear you speak. Help me let go of things from the past that hold me so I can have *"life to the full"* as you promised.

Chapter 11

Some Bible readings, based on passages Mary wrote about:
Proverbs 23:7; 2 Corinthians 10:5; Philippians 4:8; Proverbs 17:22; Romans 12:2

1. How do you respond when your dreams and desires are taken away?

2. What can you comment about the effect that the words of others have had on you? Do you notice them or think back on them as Mary did?

3. What is your vision (even in older age)? Do you seek God and wait to see what he says?

4. God has ways of encouraging us with prophetic words, pictures or Scripture verses. Are there words or pictures you have received, or encouragements you sense God has given you, that you need to look at again?

5. 'Battles and Blessings'. Have you noticed this pattern in your life? How do you cope? In your own strength or God's?

Prayer

Thank you, Jesus for the encouragement your Word brings and for the insight of other believers that have helped me over the years. Would you sharpen my hearing and vision, so I have more of your wisdom for my life; and more of your strength to fulfil your plans. I cancel every word that I have spoken over my life or that others have said, that is wrong, damaging or restrictive. I choose today to believe the truth of what you say and think about me, even if the reality of it remains to be seen.

Chapter 12

Some Bible readings, based on passages Mary wrote about:
Psalm 118:24; Romans 12:2; Proverbs 3:5; Isaiah 55:8–9; Isaiah 26:3; Joshua 1:8

1. Taking off the graveclothes (John 11:44): what do you need to step out of and what old habits do you need to change?

2. What choices do you make when you wake up in the morning? What do you fill your mind with (Facebook, TV, News, God's Word)? What changes do you need to make to alter that pattern?

3. Mary gives God all the glory. On her own she would not have been able to cope but God provided the skills, the right people at the right time and his encouraging and directional voice. What have you learnt for the next step in your life?

4. Look at 1 Thessalonians 5:16–22. There are 7 points in these verses that all speak of choice. Which ones are you learning to live in?

5. Mary shared very honestly about her journey, particularly about learning to think in godly ways and to think of herself as God sees her. Are there aspects of your life where your thinking needs to be renewed?

6. How has Mary's story challenged you about how you think and live? What changes might you need to consider?

Mary's Prayer for You

The Lord bless you and keep you

The Lord make His face shine upon you

And be gracious to you

The Lord lift up His countenance upon you

And give you peace.

(Numbers 6)